W9-DHI-732

Advance Praise for
*Wall Street Secrets for Tax-Efficient Investing:
From Tax Pain to Investment Gain*
by Robert N. Gordon with Jan M. Rosen

"Bob Gordon and Jan Rosen know that it's what you keep rather than how much you earn that really counts. This book provides an easy to read and remember menu of tax minimizing techniques and strategies. **Every taxpayer should have a copy as a guide in the never-ending joust with the revenue codes.**"

> Robert H. Stovall, CFA
> Senior Vice President and Market Strategist
> Prudential Financial

"A book every investor should have on his desk—**a very valuable guide to minimizing tax on all kinds of investments**, from retirement plans to college savings to swap contracts."

> Martin Edelston
> Publisher, *Bottom Line/Personal*

"A highly informative and original work written by the leading authority on the subject. **Destined to be a classic.**"

> Thomas J. Herzfeld
> President, Thomas J. Herzfeld Advisors

"**Understanding the growing range of tax-efficient investing alternatives is no longer an option—it's a critical element of sound financial planning.** This book is an essential tool for grasping and maximizing today's rapidly expanding menu of innovative investment choices."

    Peter Quick
    President, American Stock Exchange

"**If you hate taxes, you'll love this book!** Authors Robert Gordon and Jan Rosen reveal a catalogue of tax-cutting strategies for taxpayers and investors."

    Ed Slott, CPA
    Editor, *Ed Slott's IRA Advisor*

"**An outstanding book for investors and their advisors** on the art of tax-wise investing."

    Sidney Kess
    CPA, Attorney, Noted Lecturer, and Author

"*Wall Street Secrets for Tax-Efficient Investing* **combines Bob Gordon's deep experience with the ways of Wall Street and his practical knowledge of the intricacies of the tax code.** This is **a must-read for investors** looking for an easy to understand book on the taxation of investing."

    Richard J. Shapiro
    Tax Partner, Ernst and Young LLP

Wall Street Secrets for Tax-Efficient Investing

Also Available from Bloomberg Press

The Angel Investor's Handbook:
How to Profit from Early-Stage Investing
by Gerald A. Benjamin and Joel Margulis

Investing in Hedge Funds
by Joseph G. Nicholas

Investing in IPOs: Version 2.0
by Tom Taulli

Investing in Small-Cap Stocks: Revised Edition
by Christopher Graja and Elizabeth Ungar, Ph.D.

Stock Options—Getting Your Share of the Action:
Negotiating Shares and Terms in Incentive and Nonqualified Plans
by Tom Taulli

Tom Dorsey's Trading Tips: A Playbook for Stock Market Success
by Thomas J. Dorsey and the DWA Analysts

A complete list of our titles is available at
www.bloomberg.com/books

Attention Corporations

BLOOMBERG PRESS BOOKS are available at quantity discounts with bulk purchase for sales promotional use and for corporate education or other business uses. Special editions or book excerpts can also be created. For information, please call 609-279-4670 or write to: Special Sales Dept., Bloomberg Press, P.O. Box 888, Princeton, NJ 08542.

Wall Street Secrets for Tax-Efficient Investing

From Tax Pain to Investment Gain

Robert N. Gordon
with
Jan M. Rosen

Bloomberg Press

Princeton

© 2001 by Robert N. Gordon and Jan M. Rosen. All rights reserved. Protected under the Berne Convention. Printed in the United States of America. No part of this book may be reproduced, stored in a retrieval system, or transmitted, in any form or by any means, electronic, mechanical, photocopying, recording, or otherwise, without the prior written permission of the publisher except in the case of brief quotations embodied in critical articles and reviews. For information, please write: Permissions Department, Bloomberg Press, 100 Business Park Drive, P.O. Box 888, Princeton, NJ 08542-0888 U.S.A.

Books are available for bulk purchases at special discounts. Special editions or book excerpts can also be created to specifications. For information, please write: Special Markets Department, Bloomberg Press.

BLOOMBERG, BLOOMBERG NEWS, BLOOMBERG FINANCIAL MARKETS, OPEN BLOOMBERG, BLOOMBERG PERSONAL FINANCE, THE BLOOMBERG FORUM, COMPANY CONNECTION, COMPANY CONNEX, BLOOMBERG PRESS, BLOOMBERG PROFESSIONAL LIBRARY, BLOOMBERG PERSONAL BOOKSHELF, and BLOOMBERG SMALL BUSINESS are trademarks and service marks of Bloomberg L.P. All rights reserved.

This publication contains the authors' opinions and is designed to provide accurate and authoritative information. It is sold with the understanding that the authors, publisher, and Bloomberg L.P. are not engaged in rendering legal, accounting, investment-planning, or other professional advice. The reader should seek the services of a qualified professional for such advice; the authors, publisher, and Bloomberg L.P. cannot be held responsible for any loss incurred as a result of specific investments or planning decisions made by the reader.

First edition published 2001
1 3 5 7 9 10 8 6 4 2

Library of Congress Cataloging-in-Publication Data

Gordon, Robert N.
    Wall street secrets for tax-efficient investing: from tax pain to investment gain / Robert N. Gordon with Jan M. Rosen.
      p. cm.
    Includes index.
    ISBN 1-57660-088-2 (alk. paper)
      1. Investments–Taxation–United States. 2. Tax planning–United States.
3. Finance, Personal–United States. I. Rosen, Jan M. II. Title.

HG4910 .G669 2001
336.24'26–dc21   2001043331

Acquired and edited by Kathleen A. Peterson

Book design by Barbara Diez Goldenberg

To our families,
who graciously allowed us the long hours needed
to research and write this book

Debbie, Ali, and Evan Gordon
—R.N.G.

Albert I. Rosen, M.D.
—J.M.R.

Summary of Contents

Table of Contents

O V E R V I E W

P A R T 1

TAXABLE INVESTMENTS AND STRATEGIES FOR PROTECTING THEIR VALUE

PART 2

TAX-ADVANTAGED INVESTMENT OPPORTUNITIES

PART 3

SPECIAL SITUATIONS

P A R T 4

YOUR ANNUAL OPPORTUNITY

List of Illustrations

Preface

"...There is nothing sinister in so arranging one's affairs as to keep taxes as low as possible..."

–JUDGE LEARNED HAND

TAXES PLAY A KEY ROLE in determining your return on investment. In fact, just as Detroit has given us competing makes of automobiles, all of which will take you where you want to go, and Hollywood has produced a great variety of movies, any of which might entertain you, Wall Street has developed a great variety of competing investment products, many of which will let you make the same economic bet. But there the similarity stops. Big differences exist in the tax treatments of the various investment products, and those differences can trap the unwary, as well as offer opportunities for the savvy. As an example, in 2001 short-term profits from an S&P 500 option were taxed at 28 percent, while short-term profits from an S&P 500 index fund were taxed at 39.1 percent.

The workings of the tax code are remarkably complex, and in many ways the tax laws discourage investment more than they encourage it. Take these examples of unwary investors tripped up by the tax laws during the market downturn of 2000 and 2001:

❑ Investors who held onto appreciated securities, because selling would entail paying sizable capital gains taxes, only to see significant erosion in those positions.

❑ Mutual fund investors who saw the net asset value of their portfolios decline, but who, nevertheless, had to pay taxes on capital gains from forced distributions by the fund.

❑ Investors who realized profits in 1999 and paid taxes and then lost the same amount in 2000 but couldn't deduct the losses.

❑ Executives who delayed exercising vested stock options to avoid incurring tax liability, only to see the options become worthless, or who exercised under-water options and became liable for the alternative minimum tax—as more and more taxpayers will be in the next decade.

❑ Active traders, especially day traders, who after netting gains and losses didn't do too badly on a pretax basis, only to learn that they had run afoul of the "wash-sale" rules and actually owed more in taxes than they had made in the market.

❑ People saving for retirement who saw the value of their 401(k) or IRA plunge, and who then learned that they could not utilize a loss in a tax-deferred account.

A working knowledge of methods to manage the hidden benefits and traps within the tax laws would enable investors to solve or avoid the above issues and myriad additional tax problems they may encounter, and this knowledge is what *Wall Street Secrets for Tax-Efficient Investing* is intended to supply. For example, to avoid realizing taxable capital gains, many people continue to hold appreciated securities, thus incurring market risk. What they often do not realize is that this risk may be lessened by hedging—by using such instruments as option collars, short sales, variable forward contracts, or swaps. Even employee stock options can be protected by hedging without incurring additional tax liability.

Yet remarkably little information is readily available on the important subject of tax-efficient investing outside academic journals and Jack Crestol and Herman M. Schneider's now out-of-print work, *Tax Planning for Investors.* Drawing on my position as president of the specialized brokerage advisory firm Twenty-First Securities, I serve as an adjunct professor at New York University's Stern School of Business, where I teach courses in investment arbitrage, hedge funds, tax arbitrage, options, and derivatives pricing. From the feedback I've received from my students, many of whom work on Wall Street and are doing graduate work to increase their professional knowledge, it is quite apparent that what they particularly want is more information on taxes and tax-efficient investing.

Despite the demand for information, so little has been written on the subject of tax-efficient investing that no textbook is available. *Wall Street Secrets for Tax-Efficient Investing,* while it might help fill that gap, does not presuppose the knowledge that M.B.A. students have. Rather, it is intended for serious individual investors who want to avoid capital depletion to taxes.

Readers will find much in the book directly applicable to their own situations, and certain themes should be broadly useful. Among them are: the importance of "harvesting" losses (realizing the tax benefits of investment losses can add significantly to your return on investment); capturing long-term gains rather than ordinary income taxed at 38.6 percent; choosing the right form of equity investment for your holding period—direct ownership, exchange-traded funds, equity swaps, or futures and options; alternative forms of fixed-income investments; the basic differences in rules that affect taxable accounts and those that affect tax-advantaged plans and how to structure a tax-deferred portfolio for retirement and make the "perfect" college savings investment; and the all-important year-end strategies that investors need to whittle down tax liabilities.

Taxes are a moving target, of course, and the most recent tax law, the sweeping Economic Growth and Tax Relief Reconciliation Act of 2001, affects investors in a number of ways, as discussed throughout the book. In presenting the strategies in the book and giving examples, we generally use the top tax rate of 38.6 percent, which applies to 2002–2003. Under the 2001 tax law, rates are scheduled to gradually drop until 2006, when the top marginal rate is set at 35 percent.

This book also helps investors to become especially wary of the alternative minimum tax, which the Joint Committee on Taxation says will be tripping up more and more taxpayers as a result of the 2001 law. Other topics, such as managing employee stock options, searching for a tax-efficient mutual fund (a search that requires delving behind the name), avoiding tax traps for closely held businesses and making prudent tax elections, while crucial to people whom they affect, should be of at least passing interest to almost everyone. Breeze through the material that does not currently apply to you. There should be quite enough remaining for a hearty serving of tax savings.

Courts have long held that it is reasonable and proper to structure your financial affairs to minimize or even avoid tax liability. For example, an important reason that many people decide to buy a home instead of renting one is to take advantage of the income-tax deductions for mortgage interest and real-estate taxes. Yet, relatively few people know how best to take advantage of the tax opportunities the law offers them as investors, or how to sidestep the traps. We hope the spectrum of topics covered in these chapters will supply the practical guidance you need to enhance your financial fitness.

ROBERT N. GORDON

JAN M. ROSEN

Acknowledgments

Despite the demand for information on tax-efficient investing, so little has been written on the subject that no textbook is available, as noted. So, as a teacher, I instead distribute a lot of handouts to my students at New York University's Stern School of Business. That is how the idea of this book originated—others at NYU suggested I write it, but I had neither the skill as a writer nor the time for so ambitious an undertaking.

Then I happened to meet Kathleen Peterson, senior acquisitions editor of Bloomberg Press. She, too, saw the need for a book on tax-efficient investing, and not only for M.B.A. students but also for all individual investors, and she knew how to bring it about. Kathleen introduced me to Jan M. Rosen, who in a long career in the financial news department of *The New York Times* wrote two regular columns, *Tax Watch* and *Your Money,* and has handled a variety of editing responsibilities, including the newspaper's annual section, *Your Taxes.* Jan, too, saw the need for the book, and we agreed to work together on it.

Jan and I extend our special thanks to the staff of Twenty-First Securities, especially Charlotte Lyman, editor of the firm's quarterly newsletter *Tailored Solutions,* and Mark Fichtenbaum, tax director of the firm, for their help and support in researching a great deal of the material for this book. In addition, I want to thank my parents for making me "go figure it out" and the tax community of lawyers and accountants without whose help these ideas would not exist.

Writing the book has been arduous, but we have enjoyed doing it and hope you, as a reader, find it valuable. For additional information relevant to the topics covered in this book, I invite you to visit the Web site twenty-first.com.

R.N.G.

The Tax Code Discourages Investing More Than Encouraging It

MANY INVESTORS, ESPECIALLY new ones, have bought into a sound bite that goes like this: The nation's tax laws favor investing—long-term capital gains are taxed at 20 percent, just over half the top tax rate on earned income of 38.6 percent. But like many conclusions based on one fact, that one is wrong.

The Internal Revenue Code is enormously complex, and in many ways it discourages investing, even treats investors harshly. But if the devil is in the details, so are opportunities. This book discusses and analyzes both the traps that the tax code can spring on investors and some of the strategies that investors may legally pursue to earn top dollar, after taxes, on their holdings. This is in the spirit of the oft-quoted words of Judge Learned Hand, "Over and over again courts have said there is nothing sinister in so arranging one's affairs as to keep taxes as low as possible. Everybody does so, rich or poor; and all do right, for nobody owes any public duty to pay more than the law demands."

1

In general, the tax code discourages investing through what might be called "one-way laws." If the investor makes money, the government, which took no risk and put up no capital, demands a share. If the investor loses money, that is his problem, or mostly so; the tax laws offer little to cushion the blow. Here's an overview of some of these inequities.

Capital Gains vs. Capital Losses

AS MENTIONED, LONG-TERM capital gains—those realized on securities sold after being held more than one year—are taxable at 20 percent. However, if a taxpayer, after all her trades are netted, has a net capital loss, she may take only $3,000 of it against ordinary income. Unlike most countries, which have no limitations on taking capital losses, in the United States any excess beyond $3,000 must be carried forward to future years.

Suppose a hardworking employee had diligently saved a portion of his salary for years, depositing the money—after paying taxes, of course—into a savings account. In the year 2000 he decided to join the party that was making all his friends rich and put $100,000 of his savings into dot-com stocks, only to see his investment shrink to $20,000. So he bailed out before year-end. Could he use that $80,000 loss to offset his salary and avoid taxes for the year 2000? No, only $3,000 of the loss could be taken against ordinary income. He still had to pay taxes on the great bulk of his salary, and he has a $77,000 capital-loss carryforward. That could take many years to utilize fully. But if he had sold stocks and recognized $80,000 in profits, he would have had to pay taxes on the entire gain for the year in which it was recognized.

No Individual Carrybacks

ALTHOUGH CORPORATIONS CAN CARRY losses back as well as forward, individuals have no such choice. (On the other hand, corporations may have a separate tax problem; they are limited to five years for a carryforward, and so a corporation may not be able to utilize its losses fully.) Let's say an individual made short-term trading gains of $100,000 in 1999, but in 2000 she lost $100,000. On paper, she is even, but not after taxes. She is out about $38,400 after taxes and will be able to take a loss of $3,000 against ordinary income for the next thirty-two years, if she has no other gains or losses, reducing her tax liability by perhaps $1,200 annually.

Margin Interest

INVESTORS CAN LEVERAGE STOCK PURCHASES by borrowing up to half the cost from their brokers (the leverage can be far greater on futures, options, and certain derivatives). The interest they must pay for the loan is called margin interest. When a taxpayer has net investment income—interest, dividends, and capital gains—the margin interest is a deductible expense only to the extent it is offset by the investment income.

To compare the tax consequences of these unequal treatments of a successful margined transaction and an unsuccessful one, let's say an investor who had no other investment assets bought $100,000 worth of stock and paid margin interest on half the purchase at 8 percent. Six months later, he sold the holding for $110,000. That is a $10,000 short-term gain. After netting his interest cost of $2,000, he would pay tax on a profit of $8,000 and be left with $4,912.

3

On the other hand, let's say his stock slid, and he sold it for $90,000, incurring a $10,000 capital loss. If he already has $3,000 or more in net losses, then none of this $10,000 loss may be taken against ordinary income. So his after-tax loss is also $10,000. With no investment income, his margin interest is not deductible; therefore, he is down a total of $12,000. So, while the stock movement was 10 percent in either direction, the after-tax loss was almost two and one-half times the after-tax gain, a far cry from a level playing field. He would have to carry both his $10,000 loss and the $2,000 interest expense forward.

Nor would the tax laws allow more equitable treatment if the gains were long-term. The $10,000 gain would be taxed at 20 percent, and the investor would have to choose between carrying his margin interest deduction forward to a future year or taking it against his current capital gain, when the interest deduction would be worth only 20 percent, not 38.6 percent.

What's more, Section 265 of the Internal Revenue Code bars investors who have tax-exempt interest from municipal bonds from deducting any margin interest paid on other holdings, like those in the examples given above.

Wash Sales

AN INVESTOR WHO SELLS SHARES at a loss and then buys the same or a substantially identical stock or an option on the stock within thirty days may not, under the wash-sale rule outlined in Section 1091 of the Internal Revenue Code, claim the loss for tax purposes. However, if the investor sells the shares at a gain and then acquires the same or substantially identical shares or an option on the stock, there is no counterpart of the wash-sale rule; taxes are due on the gain. Commodity futures contracts are not covered by the wash-sale rules, and therein lies an opportunity (discussed in Chapter 1). However, any position of a straddle transaction (involving a put-option and call-option purchase on the same underlying security), which may include futures contracts, acquired after June 23, 1981, is covered by the wash-sale rule applicable to straddles (discussed in Chapter 5).

The Constructive Sales Rule

HEDGING A TRANSACTION IN A WAY that takes too much of the risk and reward out of it is considered a "constructive sale." If you make a constructive sale that produces a gain, you will owe the tax on it, even though no actual sale occurred. Only publicly traded securities are singled out for this harsh treatment. If you make a constructive sale that results in a loss, there is no offsetting rule to allow you to claim a loss. (Chapter 5 discusses constructive sales in more detail.)

Tax Consequences of Hedging with a Put

SUPPOSE AN INVESTOR WHO HAS HELD a stock long-term wants to hedge against a possible decline, so he buys a put option enabling him to sell the shares at a specified price by a specified future date. If he makes money, he has a short-term gain taxable at ordinary rates of up to 38.6 percent. If he loses money, he has a long-term loss. Because long-term losses must be taken first against long-term gains, his loss could be offsetting money that would otherwise have been taxable at only 20 percent. Thus, the tax laws give harsh and unequal treatment to investors whose hedges succeed.

Double Taxation of Dividends

THE DOUBLE TAXATION OF DIVIDENDS in the United States—first as profits at the corporate level and then at the shareholder level when part of the profits are paid out as dividends—not only discourages investing but also puts American companies at a competitive disadvantage vis-à-vis their foreign competitors. Most of the industrialized world has an integrated tax code, and as a result dividends are taxed only once. How are American companies to compete internationally when their cost of capital is so much greater than that of their overseas counterparts?

Let's say a corporation in the United States makes $1 and pays a 35 percent corporate tax. The other 65 cents is paid to the company's owner (the stockholder) as a dividend. He is in the 38.6 percent bracket and thus pays taxes of 25 cents on it. The result: The government, which is in the enviable position of getting a reward despite taking no risk, got 60 cents of the $1 the company earned, while the owner got 40 cents. After state taxes, his share could be as little as 34 cents. (And if he dies in the next few years, his estate could have to pay taxes on the 34 cents that is left of each $1 of earnings.)

Surely, the tax laws have discouraged investing. How often can an eventual return of 34 cents inspire a potential business owner to take the risks and do the hard work necessary to establish a successful corporation?

In the United Kingdom and in France, dividend recipients get a tax credit for taxes the company has already paid. In Australia and Canada dividends are tax-free to recipients, because the company that pays them has already paid taxes on the income from which shareholders were paid. America is alone among its major trading partners in not having some form of integrated tax system.

To be sure, there is a respectable body of opinion that contends that the United States ought to have only one level of taxation. In a *Wall Street Journal* opinion piece calling for "a single tax on labor income and no taxes at all on corporate income, dividends, capital gains or inheritance" (March 5, 2001), Steven E. Landsburg, a professor of economics at the University of Rochester, cited similar macroeconomic work by professors at Harvard, the Massachusetts Institute of Technology, the University of Pennsylvania, the University of Minnesota, and the University of Chicago.[1] Nevertheless, at present Americans must work with an extremely complex tax code and multiple levels of taxation. That is the reality that this book addresses.

While no rational person disputes the government's need to collect taxes to pay for the services a civilized society needs—education, police protection, national defense, the salaries of public officials, and myriad other needs—few people want to pay more than their fair share. (It is actually possible to pay extra income taxes voluntarily, but who does that?) And few would dispute the theoretical justice of a graduated income tax—those who can afford to pay more must do so. Indeed, tax-payers in the top 5 percent by income—$145,199 in 2001—are liable for 56.6 percent of taxes, according to the Joint Committee on Taxation (for further information see the illustration on the following page).

If that seems steep, one reason, arguably, is that because of the complexities of the Internal Revenue Code, in practice many upper-income taxpayers actually do pay more than their fair share; that is, more than they would if they knew how to structure investments for more favorable tax treatment. This book is intended to fill that knowledge gap.

Who Pays the Income Taxes?

Under the nation's graduated tax rates, the most affluent people pay the lion's share of the taxes. Those in the top 1 percent of income ($340,306* or more in 2001) have 17.2 percent of income and pay 35.9 percent of taxes. People with incomes of $200,000* and over have 24.5 percent of the income and pay 47.5 percent of the taxes. Below, by income levels: the percentages of all taxes paid, all income reported, and all returns filed.

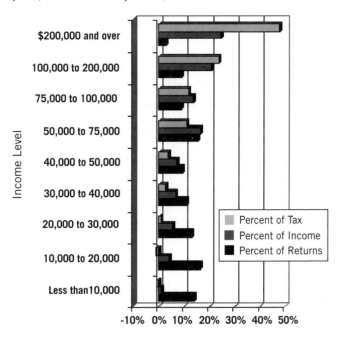

*Includes certain employer-provided and other benefits.

Source: Joint Committee on Taxation

Unmasking the Opportunities

THE INTERNAL REVENUE CODE'S traps and unequal treatment of seemingly parallel transactions can leave an investor whose trades did not turn out as hoped feeling that insult has been added to injury. However, careful study of the rules can uncover opportunities to sidestep some of the traps, and at times you can even use the maddeningly complex rules to your advantage. What follows in this book is a look at those opportunities.

PART 1

Taxable Investments and Strategies for Protecting Their Value

CHAPTER 1

Choosing Your Investment Tools Carefully

MANY WALL STREET PROFESSIONALS are fond of the adage, "You can't time the market." Perhaps not. But you can time your taxes, often for highly advantageous results. To do so, select your investment tools carefully. Wall Street's ingenuity has created many tools or investment products with which to make the same economic bet, but those products receive widely varying tax treatment. Which equity product to choose for the best after-tax returns—the subject of this chapter—depends on individual circumstances, what direction the bet is intended to take, and one's time horizon. The best tools for fixed-income investments are discussed in Chapter 4.

The Time-Horizon Factor

TYPICALLY, INDIVIDUAL INVESTORS tend to buy securities directly, regardless of how long they intend to hold them, rather than investing in options or other derivatives. In general, however,

---

Tools of Choice for Bullish Investors by Holding Period

Less than One Year

Futures or Nonequity Options

All gains and losses are treated as 60% long term and 40% short term.

One to Five Years

Equity Swaps

Cost to carry is deductible. Losses can be claimed as miscellaneous itemized deductions, not capital losses. Gains can be long term.

More than Five Years

Outright Ownership

Paper gains and losses have no tax consequences. Once an investor sells, the gain or loss is recognized for tax purposes. Investment interest expense is deductible to the extent there is investment income to offset it.

---

outright ownership is most beneficial only when an investor wants the ability to "own" the security longer than Wall Street is willing to write bets, now generally a maximum of five years.

For bullish bets of less than one year, futures and broad-based equity options (such as those on the Standard & Poor's 500 stock index) offer the greatest tax advantages and thus the greatest after-tax returns. For periods between one and five years, an equity swap is often the best choice for affluent

---

Tools of Choice for Bearish Investors by Holding Period

Less than One Year

Futures or Nonequity Options

All gains and losses are treated as 60% long term and 40% short term.

More than One Year

Buy Puts or Swaps

Cost to carry is deductible. Losses can be claimed as miscellaneous itemized deductions, not capital losses. Gains can be long term.

---

investors. For pessimistic investors, so-called 60/40 contracts are best for holding periods under one year, but LEAP (long-term equity anticipation security) puts might be best for bearish sentiments of one to five years. Here is a discussion of each of these strategies.

Long-Term Investment Tools

Direct Ownership

As most investors know, capital gains on securities held more than one year are classified as long-term and taxed at a maximum rate of 20 percent, just over half the top rate of 38.6 percent on ordinary income. (The rules are different for capital gains on small businesses, collectibles, and some real estate.) Effective in the year 2006, gains on securities acquired in 2001 or later and held more than five years can qualify for a maximum tax rate of 18 percent, pursuant to provisions of the Taxpayer Relief Act of 1997.

In addition to enjoying a favorable tax rate on long-term capital gains, investors who own securities directly enjoy the great tax advantage of deferral. That is, they can choose when to recognize their gains or losses by selling shares and let their assets grow in value until they do so. There is no tax due on paper profits.

The advantage of deferral does not necessarily hold true, however, for mutual fund shareholders. As required by federal law, when funds trade securities in their portfolios and realize gains or when they receive dividends, they must pass on those gains and dividends to their shareholders and issue a Form 1099 reporting them to the Internal Revenue Service. If the fund is held outside a tax-deferred retirement account or an IRA, a fund shareholder will generally owe taxes annually as a result. In contrast, a direct stockholder can let her portfolio keep growing until she decides to sell shares. Furthermore, people who inherit stock before 2010—and in some cases then, too—get a step-up in basis. That is, their basis is the value on the decedent's day of death, not the decedent's own basis. (See Chapter 6.)

Spiders

As an alternative to investing in an open-end mutual fund and facing an annual tax liability for gains recognized in the fund's portfolio, investors who are long-term market bulls may be well advised to invest in exchange-traded funds such as Spiders—Standard & Poor's Depositary Receipts—because they redeem in kind rather than selling holdings. A Spider is an unmanaged unit investment trust of the S&P 500 that trades on the American

Stock Exchange like a stock. It charges minimal trustee fees and has no turnover as a result of redemptions, although like any exchange-traded fund, as the index changes, it will still have to make trades that could be taxable to shareholders.

Even so, Spiders are more tax-efficient than open-end mutual funds that mimic the S&P 500, which, in turn, are generally more tax-efficient than actively managed funds. Index funds may still have to sell some holdings when faced with a high level of redemptions. If there are gains on those sales, shareholders with regular accounts, as opposed to tax-deferred accounts, must report their share of the gains, which will be subject to taxes. Conversely, exchange-traded funds, through the mechanism of redemption in kind, never sell their underlying portfolios, so shareholders are not subject to the same kind of gain. In a study issued by Morningstar in August 1998, the most recent we have seen on the subject, the average index fund with more than $2 billion in assets had an embedded gain of 36 percent, which could portend severe future problems should there be a market downturn that leads to heavy redemptions, causing the fund managers to have to sell holdings. And, of course, the bull market continued well past August 1998, so the embedded gains now are no doubt even higher.

Other Types of Exchange-Traded Funds

There are today a wide variety of tax-efficient investments similar to Spiders known as exchange-traded funds (ETFs) or "holders receipts" for specific baskets of securities. Although these investments have been available since 1993, their popularity has surged only in recent years. The Investment Company Institute (ICI), the mutual fund industry trade group, reported that at the end of January 2001, assets of exchange-traded funds were $72.1 billion, twice as much as a year earlier. The most popular, by far, of the funds is the $25.8 billion Nasdaq 100 Index Tracking Stock, an ETF known on Wall Street by its ticker symbol, QQQ. It is the most heavily traded issue on the American Stock Exchange.

Barclays Global Investors offers more than fifty ETFs, known as Barclays iShares, which had assets of $6.6 billion in January 2001, according to the ICI. They track indexes as familiar as the S&P 500 and as esoteric as a Malaysian index. The iShares are essentially mutual funds that have boards and can reinvest dividends more frequently than can unit investment trusts.

In addition to Spiders and iShares, there is a third major type of exchange-traded fund, Merrill Lynch's "HOLDRS." These are baskets of stocks, such as its Internet HOLDRS, known by the ticker symbol HHH, that are not tied to a changing index but can be exchanged for the underlying securities.

Short-Term Investment Tools

Futures and Options

Whether an investor is bullish or bearish, in short-term investments—those lasting one year or less, which normally would be taxed at up to 38.6 percent—futures and listed index options (not over-the-counter options) get better tax treatment than direct ownership of the underlying securities. Under the law, capital gains on futures and certain options are automatically treated as 60 percent long-term and 40 percent short-term, regardless of the holding period, resulting in a blended rate of 27.44 percent. Why? The proper question, actually, is: Who? And the answer is former Representative Dan Rostenkowski of Illinois, the once-powerful chairman of the House Ways and

Means Committee and a principal architect of the Tax Reform Act of 1986. Although Mr. Rostenkowski is no longer in power, his legacy as a champion of the Chicago futures and options exchanges endures.

This means short-term investors have a choice of how to be taxed—60/40 for options on the index, versus regular rates of up to 38.6 percent on short-term gains resulting from sales of mutual funds, including ETFs, which do not share in the 60/40 treatment.

Say an upper-income investor who is a near-term bull on the overall market invests in a mutual fund that mimics the S&P 500 stock index. Assuming she is right about the market's direction and sells a few months later, she will have a short-term capital gain taxable as ordinary income at 38.6 percent.

A better tool for her in terms of after-tax return on investment would be a futures contract on the index. Alternatively, she could buy a call option and sell a put option on the index with the same strike price and expiration. Because of the 60/40 rule, her blended tax rate on the profit comes to 27.44 percent (60 percent of 20 percent plus 40 percent of 38.6 percent). On a $5,000 gain, she would owe taxes of $1,372 on the futures contract, compared with $1,930 for a short-term gain taxed at 38.6 percent on the index fund, for a 29 percent tax savings, or $558.

Formerly, investors had to be careful to trade the right options for this strategy to work. However, in late December 2000, shortly before leaving office, President Bill Clinton signed a law that resulted in virtually *all* exchange-traded indexes being classified as "broad-based," and thus taxable at 60 percent long-term and 40 percent short-term capital gains. Thus, a top-bracket investor would then pay a blended rate of 27.8 percent; for 2002 and 2003, the rate is 27.44 percent.

The new definition introduced at the end of 2000 brings

index options into line with futures contracts. As noted previously, all futures contracts currently enjoy the same blended 60/40 tax rate. The definition should create a more level tax field for different types of investment vehicles. (Although there are few, if any, traded indexes that would be considered narrow-based, the law provides that options on these "narrow-based indexes" or exchange-traded funds based on the indexes will be taxed the same way as stocks and bonds, with short-term gains taxable at regular rates of up to 38.6 percent.)

Similarly, an investor who expects a downturn in the market or on a specific stock can choose from a number of investment tools. The most obvious strategy is to sell the stock short, that is, sell stock borrowed from one's broker. Then, after the price declines, the investor closes out the position, that is, repays the loan with stock purchased at current lower prices. The difference between the price of the short sale and the price to close the position is the investor's profit. The tax rub is that no matter how long the short position was open, the gain will be treated as short term, taxable at regular rates of up to 38.6 percent.

From a tax perspective, it would be better for the bearish investor to buy a long-dated put option (LEAP) on the stock. If the option is held more than a year, the gain would be treated as long term, taxable at 20 percent for most taxpayers. On a $10,000 gain, the tax on a short sale would be $3,860, or $1,860 more than the $2,000 tax that would be owed on a similar gain from a LEAP—nearly double the tax burden.

Equity Swaps

For affluent investors who qualify as swap participants (with a $3 million minimum investment and $10 million in gross assets), the best tool for a one-to-five-year holding is an equity

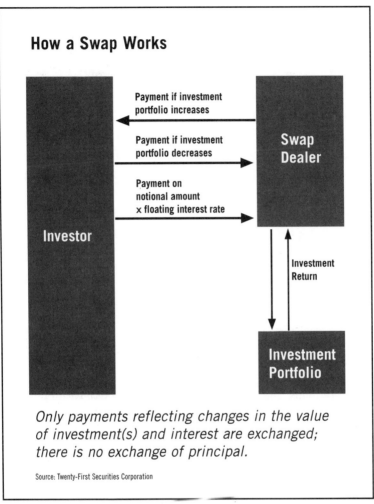

How a Swap Works

Payment if investment portfolio increases

Payment if investment portfolio decreases

Payment on notional amount x floating interest rate

Swap Dealer

Investor

Investment Return

Investment Portfolio

Only payments reflecting changes in the value of investment(s) and interest are exchanged; there is no exchange of principal.

Source: Twenty-First Securities Corporation

swap. A swap is the perfect investment vehicle because the investor has a choice of how he would like to be taxed. A swap is a contractual agreement under which two parties exchange payments based on the price changes and distributions from a security, as well as the cost to carry the security.

A swap investor retains all the upside and downside potential of the stock but gets to keep the cash that would have been tied up in the investment. The net cost of the swap is the difference between the interest earned on the dollars kept and the "interest" charged on the notional amount of the contract. (The notional value of a swap contract simply provides a tool for measurement; it is called *notional* because it is not a physical asset but is a reference to an investment in an asset of a specified amount.) Under law, payments made or received under the contract are ordinary income or loss, but if the contract is terminated early, any payments made upon early termination are capital in nature. Because of this, it is possible to choose your tax treatment—ordinary income or capital gains or losses—*after* you know the result.

In cases of a loss, you would choose to take an ordinary loss against salary, rather than a capital loss, because capital losses are quarantined and limited. If the position is profitable, you would terminate early and get a long-term gain taxed at 20 percent. Thus, you would keep 80 percent of your winners and lose only 60 cents of any dollar lost.

The swap contract can be written so that you make periodic payments for not only the cost to carry the position but also any interim losses, and you generally get to take ordinary deductions for those payments. (One word of caution: These deductions are miscellaneous itemized deductions that are allowed only to the extent they exceed 2 percent of adjusted gross income, so you should review your particular tax situation carefully to determine whether you will be able to deduct all or part of the financing costs.)

The contract, however, can stipulate that all payments and receipts with respect to dividends and price movement will be deferred until the end of the swap agreement. This allows the investor to practice "dividend arbitrage," that is, defer taking the dividend and instead receive it as a capital gain taxable at 20 percent when exiting the swap as it matures. The trade-off, of course, is that by deferring receipt, the investor has not been able to put the money to work as soon as she would have had she accepted payment equal to the dividend.

As the swap nears maturity, the investor has a choice. If the stock has increased in value after a year or longer, he can end the agreement and recognize a long-term capital gain. If the stock has decreased, the investor can simply make the final payment on the swap and take the tax deduction for it.

Thanks to the ordinary deductions for losses, a swap investor who makes a bad market call can get a far greater tax benefit than an investor who sells directly owned shares at a loss. Remember that capital losses must be taken first against capital gains. Say an investor has $1 million of net capital losses. Because only $3,000 of net capital losses a year can be taken against ordinary income, with the rest carried forward, it could take many years for this investor to utilize them all for tax purposes, if indeed they could ever be entirely utilized.

Under the tax code, it is possible to take a swap position on an equity, index, debt security, or commodity, and the strategy may be utilized with either a long or short position in the underlying property. You cannot hold a hedge fund or mutual fund in a swap and get the tax benefits, because of the constructive ownership rules. However, a swap could probably work on an individually managed account. As noted previously, because the minimum for a swap position is typically $3 million, many small investors are priced out of the market. Further, the law requires anyone entering into a swap position to have a minimum of $10 million in gross assets. Because the law says "gross assets," the magic number can be reached by leveraging positions. Still, this is not a tool for investors of modest means.

For those who qualify, however, a swap, because it is personally tailored, can offer great flexibility as well as tax benefits. Here is an example of a typical swap transaction:

Say a sixty-year-old business owner intends to sell her business in two or three years. She is bullish on the market and does not want to have to wait to invest the proceeds she anticipates from the sale of the business. A swap is an ideal way to take a position on the market now. So, on October 15, 2001, she visits her investment banker and enters into a total-return swap with a notional amount of $10 million on the performance of the S&P 500.

During the three-year life of the swap she will make interest-based payments to the swap dealer (the investment banker) on $10 million, the notional amount. At the end, if the S&P index has increased by 20 percent, she will terminate the swap and realize a $2 million long-term gain taxable at 20 percent. (Swap profits are treated as long-term gains, provided the swap has been in existence at least twelve months.)

If she has been mistaken in her market judgment and the S&P 500 declines by 15 percent, she would have to make a payment of $1.5 million, but that blow would be mitigated on an after-tax basis because the interim payment and the final payment to the dealer should qualify as ordinary deductions worth 38.6 percent.

Let's say that she indeed has sold her business before the termination of the swap, and she is still bullish on the market and hopes to live many years on portfolio income and eventually leave her portfolio to her children or grandchildren. She would take the proceeds from the business sale and invest them in the market. She could simply buy an ETF, but with $10 million, she might prefer a direct stock investment because she could choose when (and if) to recognize gains, and she could harvest any losses.

Alternatively, let's say when she sells the business she is considering a "sabbatical," say traveling a year or so, and then possibly opening a new business for which she would need start-up capital. She could enter into another swap contract and decide later whether to buy stocks, open a new business, or do some of each. The Wall Street house that is on the other side of the swap can write the contract, in effect extending her credit, because of her sizable gross assets.

There is one downside to a swap: Under the contract, the expiration date is certain. The investor cannot simply stay with a winner but must end the agreement and report the gain. This is particularly disadvantageous for an investor who does not want to exit the position. However, under the tax bill President George W. Bush signed into law in June 2001, one disadvantage of this forced realization of profit is scheduled to be eased. Under the previous law, when an investor died, his heirs got what could be a big income-tax break, known as a step-up in basis, meaning that the estate would not owe any tax on the capital gains that occurred during his lifetime.

But in the new law, one trade-off for the rate cuts and other tax breaks provided is that the step-up in basis at death will be modified, once the estate tax is eliminated in 2010.

Say an investor who bought $10,000 worth of stock forty years earlier dies before 2010, leaving the shares to his daughter. At the time of his death the shares are worth $1 million. Other assets are used to pay estate taxes, and after the estate is probated and settled, his daughter inherits and sells the shares, which by then are worth $1.1 million. Her taxable capital gain is $100,000, and capital gains of $990,000 have totally escaped taxation. But if he dies in 2010, depending on the circumstances, her taxable gain could be as much as $1,090,000. That year an estate's first $1.3 million of asset appreciation can be allocated among beneficiaries, who will get a step-up in basis as before, and an additional $3 million can go to a spouse. However, after the first $4.3 million (or after the first $1.3 million if there is no surviving spouse), the market value of the shares on the day the owner dies will be used as the beneficiaries' basis in the stock. In some cases there could be adjustments, for example, if the owner had unused loss carryforwards.

TO MAKE THE MOST TAX-EFFICIENT INVESTMENT possible give careful consideration to how long you expect to keep a holding, for your time horizon is as important as your outlook for the market or the particular issue you are buying in terms of after-tax returns. Typically, individual investors tend to buy stocks directly, and that is just the thing to do if you anticipate keeping a security many years for long-term growth, because that growth will not be taxed until you do decide to sell, and of course the timing of the sale is up to you. But if you are making a short-term investment or one of one to five years, the other investment techniques described in this chapter offer greater tax-efficiency.

CHAPTER 2

The How and When
of Harvesting
Your Losses

TAXABLE INVESTORS WHO FOCUS on realizing capital losses only at year-end are leaving a lot of performance on the table. Knowing how—and when—to harvest losses can significantly mitigate the damage losses can do to your portfolio.

Despite the importance of loss harvesting as part of disciplined year-round portfolio management, the practice, although known to investment professionals and academicians, has received little public attention. In a recent study, Robert Arnott, managing partner of First Quadrant, L.P.; Andrew L. Berkin, Ph.D., associate director; and Jia Ye, Ph.D., conducted 400 Monte Carlo simulations, each with a universe of 500 assets.[1] They thus generated a twenty-five-year history of monthly returns subject to a 35 percent average tax rate for each asset. They found that the excess return generated from monthly loss harvesting was 80 (after-tax) basis points annually.

Pointing to the premium earned by loss harvesting, the authors wrote in the *Journal of Wealth Management,* "Over a

25-year span, assuming modest 8 percent returns on stocks, we earn an average of almost 2,000 basis points of cumulative alpha [overperformance versus the market] just from harvesting the losses. And that's *net* of all of the taxes that you would face at the end of the period for liquidating the portfolio. It's a very important source of after-tax alpha, and it's both reliable and predictable."

Those results, incidentally, are in line with those of a 1999 study by David M. Stein and Premkumar Narasimhan, both of Parametric Portfolio Associates, a Seattle-based investment firm that specializes in tax-efficient investing. They found a tax-management alpha ranging from 0.7 percent to 1.5 percent a year, on average, over a ten-year period for a large-capitalization domestic equity portfolio, assuming average market returns of 4 percent to 15 percent.

Further, we are aware of a long/short hedge fund that proactively harvests losses. It has generated almost 50 cents in net losses for every dollar invested, thereby lowering its investors' tax bills, because the investors can use those losses to offset other portfolio gains.

But that is far from typical. Studies have shown—as most brokers can confirm—that investors tend to sell winners and hold losers in the hope that the losers will come back at least to the price at which they bought them. The explanation may be a psychological difficulty that many people have in admitting error. But for both maximum investment performance and tax efficiency, it is better to sell a portfolio's losers and hold the winners. As the First Quadrant study pointed out, one source of taxable mismanagement is unnecessary capital gains realization.

"Unrealized capital gains in a portfolio are effectively a 'free loan' of deferred tax obligations from the government," the authors wrote. Therefore, it makes sense to hold onto winners as long as they have strong fundamentals. When a stock appears overvalued, rather than selling it alone, a sound tax practice is to sell a loser at the same time, thereby harvesting a loss that can offset the gain on the winner. What's more, the authors found in their simulations that harvesting losses systematically each month—not only when losses were needed to offset gains—increased returns by 60 to 100 basis points a year. Fortunately for individual investors, today's numerous online portfolio tracking programs from brokerage houses and organizations like Morningstar and Bloomberg make it easy to stay on top of one's portfolio and harvest losses.

Here are the methods investors may utilize in realizing losses in their portfolios, along with the pitfalls to avoid along the way.

Harvesting Winners and Losers

WHEN A PORTFOLIO HAS BOTH unrealized winners and unrealized losers, it is advantageous to harvest them together. Because capital losses can offset capital gains dollar for dollar, an investor who believes a winner has had its run can sell it and avoid tax on the capital gain by selling a holding with an equivalent loss. Under the tax code, short-term losses are taken first against short-term gains, and then long term losses are taken against long-term gains. Finally, the net short-term gain or loss is taken against the net long-term gain or loss. If that results in a net capital loss, up to $3,000 a year can be taken against ordinary income (such as salaries, dividends, or interest). Losses in excess of $3,000 can generally be carried forward to future years to be taken first against capital gains and then against ordinary income (with the same $3,000 annual limit).

From a tax perspective, capital losses are most useful when applied against ordinary income or short-term gains, because they are taxed at higher rates than long-term (more than one year) capital gains, which are taxed at a maximum rate of 20 percent. That rate is just over half the top rate on ordinary income in 2002 and 2003 of 38.6 percent. The extent to which you have ordinary income and short-term gains to offset is an important factor to consider when deciding whether to recognize a portfolio loss.

Avoiding Wash Sales

PORTFOLIOS WITH PAPER LOSSES do not always have paper gains that neatly offset them, and often investors still have faith in a holding that is under water. So the problem becomes how to have it both ways: recognize the loss for tax purposes but keep the holding. That is possible, but investors must be mindful of the so-called wash-sale rules in Section 1091 of the Internal Revenue Code, which mandate that the loss cannot be recognized for tax purposes if the same or substantially identical new shares are purchased within thirty-one days of realizing the loss. Various updates to the rules have been made to include wash purchases from unprofitable short sales and the reestablishment of successor positions using options.

Fortunately, there are ways to operate within the wash-sale rules and keep the same economic exposure, but first let's look at the more traditional methods employed by investors and often recommended by investment advisers. These methods may well change how much you make or lose.

❏ **The first choice** is to sell the stock and not reinvest for thirty-one days. Doing this, the investor would sacrifice any appreciation on the security during that time but conversely would be protected from any further slide in its price.

❏ **A second choice** is to sell the loss position and purchase another security that you believe will "act like" the original holding. Here the investor must weigh the viability of the possible substitutes. High-grade bonds seem the most homogeneous as an asset class and the easiest to swap between, while small-cap equities seem the least interchangeable. Even blue-chip stocks in the same industry are not necessarily surrogates for each other. Within an industry, there are often both winners and losers.

Purchasing a bond of a different issuer, or purchasing a different bond of the same issuer but with a different interest rate and maturity, should allow the investor to deduct the loss and avoid running afoul of the wash-sale rule. He or she might consider selling the bond to establish the loss for tax purposes and then buying it back thirty-one days later. The waiting period is crucial. If an investor buys the same (or a substantially identical) security within thirty days before or after the date of the sale, the transaction is classified as a "wash sale," and the loss on the sale cannot be deducted, although it is incorporated into the cost basis of the security bought with the proceeds of the sale.

Doubling Up on Shares

An alternative long favored by tax advisers and portfolio managers has been to "double up." This involves buying an equal parcel of the security that has the unrealized loss and holding those shares along with the first lot for the requisite thirty-one days. At the end of the thirty-one-day waiting period, the same number of shares is sold, and the tax lot chosen is the first parcel of shares. This identification must be made with the broker. It should appear on the sales confirmation, and it could read "against shares purchased (original shares' purchase date)." Of course, while technically crafted to travel the wash-sale rule safely, doubling up means the investor assumes twice the risk/reward. Further, the investor must have idle cash available for such a purchase or have other holdings he can sell with little worry or tax consequence. Consider the following example in which the stock does not move in thirty-one days:

9/12/90:	1,000 shares purchased at $50
Risk:	1,000 shares from 9/12/90–3/15/01
3/15/01:	Another 1,000 shares purchased at $10
Risk:	2,000 shares from 3/15/01–4/20/01
4/20/01:	Sell 1,000 shares at $10, delivering shares purchased at $50, realizing a $40 per-share loss
Risk:	1,000 shares thereafter

Doubling Up Forward Conversion

Arguably, a far more effective approach that does not entail any additional risk is the doubling up forward conversion that enables the investor to hedge all the risk of the second lot of shares. It, too, requires additional capital, but the investor can earn a reasonable rate of return on that capital. Under this strategy, the investor purchases additional shares of the under-water holding, doubling the original holding, and buys a put (an option to sell the security by a specific date) on the new shares and sells a call (an option to buy the security by a specific time) with the same strike price as the put on the new shares. This transaction enables the investor to recognize the loss while avoiding both a wash sale and any additional market risk.

Here is an example, based on the one above, that would keep the net exposure at 1,000 shares:

3/15/01: Additional 1,000 shares purchased at $10
Sell a call option with a $10 strike price
Buy a put option with a $10 strike price
Both have a 4/20/01 expiration
Net Risk: Only the first 1,000 shares from 3/15/01–4/20/01, instead of 2,000 shares

A transaction that has no risk should earn the risk-free rate of return, not zero. This is the equivalent of earning interest on capital while being invested for thirty-one days, so to complete the example, the value of the call sold should be more than the cost of the put, netting an annualized profit at expiration. If the shares are above $10, you can be sure they will be called away. If the shares are below $10, then the investor exercises his put to sell at $10. Either way the exit price has been contracted at inception. Of course, the investor delivers the shares purchased at $50 on September 12, 1990, to close the transaction, realizing a $40 per-share loss.

We recommend selling calls and buying puts that have the same strike price and expiration date (a forward conversion). This strategy can (and should) be used all year but cannot be put into place after November 30 for any given year because the necessary thirty-one days must occur before year-end.

Equity Swaps

Traditionally, investment advisers thought that an investor with a sizable position could sell shares and immediately reestablish the position by entering a swap (discussed in Chapter 1) without running afoul of the wash-sale rules. This belief was grounded on the basis that the rules applied only to stock and securities and that swaps were not "securities." However, on December 29, 2000, the wash-sale rules were amended to include contracts that settled in cash or property other than the stock sold.

This amendment might cause swaps to be captured by the wash-sale rules, which disallow taking a loss if the investor enters into a contract to buy the same or substantially similar securities within thirty days. When an effective method of avoiding taxes comes to Washington's attention, there are frequently moves to halt it. For example, "selling short against the box" (a technique discussed in Chapter 5) had traditionally been the favored way to lock in profits without selling the shares until Estée Lauder and her son Ronald Lauder used it successfully when the family sold its cosmetics empire to the public in late 1995. Following public outcry at the transaction, the Clinton administration proposed regulations that were subsequently adopted to curb use of the strategy.

Another disadvantage to swaps is that they are available only to those with larger positions (as most swap dealers have minimums of $3 million to $5 million). We have found that the hedged double-up transaction discussed above is more widely embraced by the tax community, and thus we have seen the most activity there. Significantly, however, a swap can be accomplished until the last day of the year, unlike the forward conversion described in the preceding section, which must be entered into by November 30. Note also that if you want a transaction with no built-in time limit, an equity swap may not be appropriate, because swap dealers are generally willing to write swap contracts for a maximum of five years.

Writing Puts

Another transaction that is widely used, even though it alters the economic position of the investor, is to sell the depressed stock so that you can harvest the loss and, assuming you still like the stock, immediately write a put option on it. If you buy the stock back or buy a call option, you will run afoul of the wash-sale rule, but if you write a put that retains some element of risk (the government has not specified how much) you have a good chance of being able to buy the stock back at or near the price for which you sold it.

As the writer—that is, the seller—of a put option, you are obligated to purchase the stock if the holder—that is, the buyer—exercises the put. As long as the stock remains below the strike price of the put on the expiration date, the put will be exercised. If the stock reverses course and climbs, you have a small compensation prize, the money you received for writing the put, but you will have missed out on the appreciation. Clearly there is some risk in this strategy, and that is necessary to avoid running afoul of the wash-sale rules.

Say, for example, you bought a stock at 20, and ten months later it has fallen to 8. You could sell it and write a thirty-one-day put with a strike price of 8, pocketing a premium of 1. Over the next month the stock slips to 7. There can be no doubt that the holder of the put will sell you the stock at 8, and both sides will be happy. But if instead of falling to 7, the stock had suddenly recovered and climbed to 15, the option would have expired worthless, and you would have missed the stock's appreciation, so economically your loss-harvesting effort would have backfired.

The Internal Revenue Service has ruled that the writing of the put will violate the wash-sale rules if the strike price of the put is so far in excess of the stock's price at the time that it was written that it is almost certain that the put will be exercised. In other words, the IRS will not tolerate a deep-in-the-money put, but an at-the-money put or an out-of-the-money put ought to allow the option writer to avoid being tripped up by the wash-sale rule. In that case, however, the investor will forfeit the appreciation in excess of the strike price of the put. Investors planning to use this strategy might consider using "European-style" options, which are exercisable only on their due date, to avoid the early exercise of the put.

Choosing a Harvesting Method

UNREALIZED LOSSES ARE AN ASSET that must be utilized in the drive to increase tax efficiency in your investment portfolio. To achieve the highest after-tax returns with the least amount of risk, you must fight the natural inclination to hold onto a loser in the often-forlorn hope it will bounce back and strive to harvest your losses in a regular, disciplined way. When choosing among the harvesting methods described above, ask yourself two questions:

1 Does the transaction create any incremental and unintended overall portfolio risks?
2 Does the cost of the transaction justify the anticipated tax benefit?

Answering these two questions will most often lead you to the doubling up forward conversion or the simultaneous purchase of a reasonably similar security, and away from the traditional approach involving doubling up.

First Quadrant's 400 simulations encompassed a wide range of market conditions, from bull markets as good as (or better than) the most recent twenty-five-year span to bear markets as bad as 1929 to 1953, a twenty-five-year span in which the price of domestic equities fell. In each simulation, the authors monitored two portfolios: a buy-and-hold portfolio and a tax-advantaged portfolio. In the buy-and-hold portfolio, the only transactions that occurred were those forced by corporate actions like takeovers and mergers. The tax-advantaged portfolio was swept every month, and all assets with losses were sold and immediately bought back.

"For each month," the authors wrote, "we ask the simple question: If we were to liquidate both portfolios *right now,* how does the tax-advantaged portfolio compare to the passive buy-and-hold benchmark, after all remaining taxes have been paid?" Even after twenty-five years, they found, the tax savings of the tax-advantaged portfolio were around 0.5 percent a year, "*an alpha that most active managers cannot add reliably even before taxes.*"

The median twenty-five-year gain from loss harvesting was nearly 20 percent, or about 80 basis points a year. "Despite the fact that the simulation will cover scenarios with splendid returns and scenarios with awful returns," they wrote, "the range is surprisingly tight: from 60–100 basis points per annum [are] added through loss harvesting. Interestingly, the best value-added typically comes from the scenarios with *lackluster* returns: The opportunities to harvest losses, over a span of many years, are best if market returns are poor."

EACH DECENT-SIZED LOSS in a portfolio needs to be taken. In a particular situation, the hope that a stock will bounce back may not be a forlorn one. However, as the studies have shown, overall, investors who do not follow an active discipline of loss harvesting are leaving almost a full percentage point of return (80 basis points) on the table each year.

CHAPTER 3

Techniques for

Utilizing Your Losses

MANY INVESTORS FEEL FORCED to retreat after incurring a big loss. Say an investor bought 1,000 shares of Yahoo! at $238 a share late in 1999, at the height of the Internet feeding frenzy. After more than a year of waiting for the stock to bounce back, he was sitting on a loss of more than $200,000.

If he happens to have big gains in his portfolio that he has been reluctant to take because of the tax liability that would result, here is his opportunity. Capital losses, after all, can offset capital gains dollar for dollar, so he can bail out of Yahoo! and recognize an offsetting amount of gains tax-free.

But suppose that instead of paper gains in his portfolio, he has more Internet stocks that have headed south. He can take only $3,000 of net capital losses against ordinary income this year.[1] Anything in excess of $3,000 must be carried forward to future years. He might have to live to be a centenarian to take all his losses against ordinary income.

Since most individual capital losses are subject to the

$3,000 annual limitation, it is good news that you can make investments that will make it possible to utilize capital losses now. Here is a discussion of those investments.

Turning the Capital Loss into Interest Expense

PEOPLE WHO HAVE SIZABLE NET capital losses that they cannot deduct immediately but who have investment income such as interest and dividends can take an immediate deduction if they convert their losses into an investment interest expense, which is deductible to the extent it is matched by investment income. As surprising as this conversion may sound, there are a variety of perfectly valid and profitable leveraged transactions that can achieve it, allowing you to utilize losses instead of having to carry them forward.

In making these transactions, investors must consider two cash flows: capital gains and the interest expense involved in making the investment. You could incur the necessary interest expense by purchasing stock on margin, provided the stock rises, but with stock investments, the necessary capital gain is far from assured. An investor needs to be more certain of getting the capital gain, and the following suggestions are intended to provide that certainty.

For example, consider the Yahoo! investor again. If he entered into a transaction that made $20,000 pretax that manifested itself as a $200,000 gain and $180,000 in carrying charges, the gain would be offset by the Yahoo! loss, and thus it would be tax-free, while the expenses should be deductible investment expenses, provided he had other portfolio income. So a $20,000 pretax profit netted more than $91,000 after tax.

Short Sales

Say you sell a stock short at $50—that is, you sell borrowed shares with the expectation of covering the loan by buying similar shares at a lower cost later. The next day the stock pays a $2 dividend and goes ex-dividend to $48. At that point, you cover the short at $48.

By observing the flow of the certificate in the diagram on the following page, you can see that there appear to be two investors who "own" the shares—the original holder who lent the shares and the buyer of the shares that were sold short. The issuer pays the dividend to the owner of record, the new buyer. You, as the short seller, owe money equal to the dividend to the investor from whom you borrowed the certificates. So you make an "in lieu of" payment to the lender. This short dividend expense is treated as an investment expense.

As a result of this transaction, you have two things: a $2 capital gain, because you sold the stock at $50 and covered the short at $48, and a $2 expense for the dividend. You should also receive a short-interest rebate, as shown in the illustration of how a short sale works. If the Yahoo! investor used this strategy and sold short 100,000 shares of the $50 stock described above, the resultant gain would nearly offset his loss on Yahoo! He would also have a $200,000 expense on the dividend payment that he could take against investment income like interest and dividends, thereby avoiding tax on that income.

Until 1985 this technique could be used with any security. However, in that year Congress passed a law requiring the short seller to be short a stock forty-six days to be able to deduct the "in lieu of" dividend payment; for a shorter period, the payment must be capitalized. But there are still several assets that you

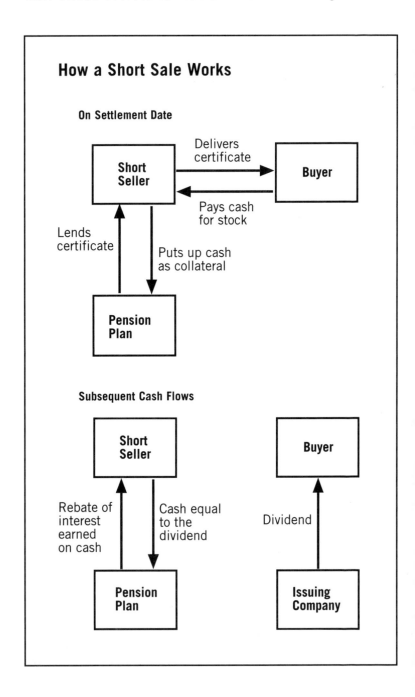

How a Short Sale Works

On Settlement Date

Short
Seller

Delivers
certificate

Buyer

Pays cash
for stock

Lends
certificate

Puts up cash
as collateral

Pension
Plan

Subsequent Cash Flows

Short
Seller

Buyer

Rebate of
interest
earned
on cash

Cash equal
to the
dividend

Dividend

Pension
Plan

Issuing
Company

can use in "overnight" transactions because they are not securities paying dividends but are payments that are characterized differently, notably Monthly Income Preferred Securities (MIPS), partnership interests, and bonds trading flat (that is, without accrued interest).

Monthly Income Preferred Securities

One form of publicly traded security that offers a potential for profit while creating both interest deductions and capital gains (for federal income tax purposes) while short is Monthly Income Preferred Securities, or MIPS. These are preferred shares that throw off monthly payments and are issued by a special-purpose subsidiary formed exclusively to sell the securities and lend the proceeds to the parent company. Although they trade on the stock exchange, under the tax laws they are classified as debt. Therefore, the payments they make are interest, not dividends.

Because of this classification, investors can use MIPS in short sales without running afoul of the forty-six-day rule. In fact, the period can be as short as one day. The investor shorts the MIPS—Texaco is one issuer—before the payment distribution date and makes an "in lieu of" payment equal to the distribution. The price of the security should drop by a corresponding amount (plus or minus any movement in market price), creating a potential short-term capital gain. The "in lieu of" payment should constitute a deductible investment expense.

Flat Bonds

Investors may also use "flat" bonds to generate profit while creating investment interest deductions and capital gains for federal income tax purposes. Typically, bond prices reflect only principal, but for a flat bond the quoted price reflects both principal and accrued interest. Most bonds that trade flat in the United States do so because they are not paying interest and therefore would not be of use in this strategy. Although there are some exceptions to that rule, it may be easier to short bonds issued in other countries, such as Australia, where all bonds trade flat. The investor is not usually exposed to currency risk because the short sale produces Australian dollars that are used to repurchase the bonds to close the short position and to make the coupon payment. However, currency fluctuations are possible, even overnight, and could complicate matters. Any gain or loss that is attributable to bond-market movements is capital in nature, but any that is attributable to currency movements is ordinary and thus would not offset capital gains or losses.

In flat-bond trades, the short sale is used, and the forty-six-day rule does not apply to bonds. The short sale is made over the record date for a coupon payment, and the short seller must make an "in lieu of" payment equal to the coupon. The price of the bond should drop by a corresponding amount (plus or minus any movement in market price), creating the potential for a short-term capital gain. The "in lieu of" payment, again, should constitute a deductible interest expense.

For example, let's say a bond of the ABC Company is trading flat at $80. The bond has a 14 percent coupon, and a semiannual interest payment of $7 per bond will be made to bondholders on the record date. An investor who wants to generate capital gains to offset losses in her portfolio sells the bond short on the assumption that the bond will decline further after the price adjusts to reflect the $7 interest payment.

If there are no other changes in market value, the ABC Company's bond should decline to $73. The investor can buy the issue at that price to close the short position, thereby generating a short-term capital gain of $7 per bond. She will also have to make a $7 "in lieu of" payment per bond, which should qualify as an income-tax deduction, provided she has investment income.

Investors generally need no cash outlays to do this transaction. Although the margin rules require collateral against short sales, assets in the account may provide sufficient collateral. The amount of collateral would depend on the liquidity and credit ratings of the bonds. Generally, an investor would have to put up a cash margin of 30 percent to 50 percent of the value of the bonds or securities of sufficient value to use as margin for the short sale.

Earning Interest as a Capital Gain Equals Tax-Free Income

ONE WAY TO EARN INTEREST as a capital gain is to buy a bond mutual fund after its last dividend payment and sell it before it pays another dividend. The difference in price caused by the fund's getting "pregnant" is built-up interest, but it is captured as a capital gain when the investor gets out before the dividend is paid. The fund must make the dividend payment to distribute the interest it has earned.

There are other opportunities that will produce interest as a capital gain, as long as you don't buy the securities for the investment from someone who markets them as creating gains. Sound strange? It is, but the Internal Revenue Code's conversion rules catch you if your return is from the use of money and the investment was marketed to you as creating capital gains. In contrast, an investor who just happens to make an investment that has the same result, however unintentionally, is not tripped up by the conversion rules.

Still other forms of investment available to people who need capital gains to offset capital losses are the senior preferred stock issued by several closed-end funds (discussed in detail in Chapter 4) and leveraged investments in stocks whose dividends are a return of capital. Such investments create gains on the sale rather than currently taxed dividends.

The appeal of these transactions is that investors get long-term gains taxed at 20 percent rather than interest taxed at 38.6 percent, and for investors with losses, either a short- or long-term gain is offset by those losses, so that it would not be taxable.

THE LOSS-UTILIZATION STRATEGIES we have described in this chapter—turning a capital loss into an interest expense, selling short MIPS or flat bonds, and timing the purchase and sale of mutual fund shares around the fund's dividend payment—should be viewed as making the most of your assets. Most investors wouldn't see an existing capital loss as an asset but that is exactly what they have, an asset that can be used to capture interest tax-free or to create a deduction where one would not have existed.

CHAPTER 4

Smart Choices for

Fixed-Income Holdings

The Obvious Approach
to Reducing the Tax Bite

MANY INCOME-ORIENTED INVESTORS take an obvious approach to reducing the tax bite on their holdings: They buy tax-exempt municipal bonds ("munis") because the yield for anyone in the middle or upper tax brackets is generally greater on triple-A-rated munis than the after-tax yield on a Treasury security of comparable maturity.

But buying munis may not be the best approach. For one thing, under a little-known provision of the Internal Revenue Code (Section 265), investors who have purchased securities on margin—that is, borrowed funds from their brokers to buy those securities—may not be able to deduct the cost of the interest that they must pay their brokers if there are tax-exempt securities in their portfolios. That is true even if the munis are in one account and the margin interest was incurred in another.

Some Less Obvious Alternative Approaches

EVEN INCOME-ORIENTED INVESTORS who do not have any margin interest may find there are far less obvious alternatives to munis that will provide greater returns on an after-tax equivalency basis. For example, by investing in the senior preferred stock of a handful of closed-end funds, you can capture what is essentially interest, which would normally be taxable at ordinary income rates, as a long-term gain taxable at only 20 percent. Since munis normally pay relatively low yields, the 80 percent of the preferreds' gain that you get to keep after taxes is likely to be greater. You might also find other opportunities such as pre-refunded, tax-exempt municipal bonds and Treasury and savings bonds that are sold with protection against inflation.

Senior Preferred Issues of Certain Closed-End Funds

IT IS POSSIBLE TO CAPTURE what is essentially interest income as a long-term gain, which is taxable at 20 percent, instead of as interest for which the tax rates are as high as 38.6 percent. How? The senior preferred stock issued by several closed-end funds that have significant unrealized capital gains pays out much of its returns as long-term capital gains. Currently, these preferred issues also seem to yield more than their triple-A status would imply. The senior preferred shares, which are intended by the funds to leverage the return on the common shares (because preferred shares function more like debt than equity), are attractive because the funds use them to realize and distribute some of their capital gains to shareholders through dividend payments.

Portfolios Are Rated Triple-A

A sizable portion of the quarterly dividends paid to shareholders qualifies for long-term-gain treatment. What's more, the entire fund portfolio, which typically is four to five times the size of the preferred issue, is pledged to secure repayment of the senior preferred. The portfolios are rated triple-A, and redemptions are mandatory should these issues be downgraded. These low-risk securities may be suitable for both individuals in high tax brackets and corporations with capital losses. (Unlike individuals, corporations cannot carry losses forward indefinitely; they have only five years to utilize their losses.)

Only four closed-end funds offer these securities as of this writing, and all trade on the New York Stock Exchange: General American Investors, the Gabelli Equity Trust, the Gabelli Global Multimedia Trust, and the Royce Value Trust. (These securities may also be appropriate for investors who need capital gains to offset capital losses, as Chapter 3 discusses.)

An Example of How They Work

Using the Royce Value Trust's cumulative preferred stock as an example, highlights as of July 2001, when the shares were trading at $25.33 a share and paying a tax-advantaged dividend of 7.3 percent, included the following:

❑ A significant portion of the dividends is subject to the long-term capital gain tax rate of 20 percent. From 1995 through 1999, approximately 72 percent of the dividends were long-term capital gains.

❑ A 7.3 percent dividend ($25 par value) is equivalent to an ordinary-income yield of 11.18 percent for taxpayers in the top federal bracket of 38.6 percent, based on 72 percent of the dividend being taxed at the long-term capital gains rate of 20 percent and the other 28 percent of the dividend being taxed as ordinary income in the top regular rate of 38.6 percent. By comparison, ten-year triple-A-rated municipal bonds were yielding 4.43 percent on average during the same period, and the ten-year Treasury note was yielding 5.14 percent.

❑ Preferred shares totaling $165 million had first claim on assets exceeding $864 million, for a coverage of 524 percent—that is, the assets were more than five times as great as the value of the preferred shares. Redemption at $25 a share is mandatory if the issue's rating falls below triple-A or coverage falls below 200 percent.

To be sure, these issues, while low risk, are not risk-free. If interest rates should soar, prices of all fixed-income investments like these will fall. Or if rates plunge, the issues could be called, meaning investors must sell them back to the issuers. Or if the stock market skids, the value of the assets held by the funds would be likely to erode. That, in turn, would endanger the credit rating, leading to redemption at par.

Still, at present, these issues are attractive for income-oriented investors who would rather have long-term gains taxed at 20 percent than interest taxed at 38.6 percent, and they are especially attractive for investors who have some portfolio losses, which would offset either a short- or long-term gain so that it would not be taxable.

Munis That Are Virtually Tax-Free "Treasuries"

ANOTHER ATTRACTIVE POSSIBILITY for bond-market investors who want the safety of Treasury securities is pre-refunded, tax-exempt municipal bonds. These issues provide safety equal to Treasuries and pay a higher yield than the after-tax yield on Treasuries.

How Pre-Re's Are Created

Pre-refunded bonds, or pre-re's, as they are known, are created when state and local governments seeking to lock in lower interest expenses effectively refinance bonds before their call dates. Because a bond cannot be redeemed before its call date, the issuer establishes an account dedicated to paying the interest and principal on the outstanding bond until the call date. The account is typically invested in Treasury securities. The result is a pre-refunded municipal bond with the same safety as a Treasury bond.

Pre-re's still enjoy the tax-exempt status of regular municipal bonds. Although their nominal yield is lower than the yield on Treasuries, the net return for an upper-income investor is greater on these munis, because Treasuries are taxable at the federal level. If a Treasury yielded 4.17 percent, an investor in the 38.6 percent bracket would have only 2.57 percent after taxes. When a Treasury was yielding that in July 2001, pre-refunded munis of comparable maturity could be purchased at yields of 3.3 percent—equivalent to a taxable yield of 5.37 percent.

The Safety Factor of Tax-Free Treasuries

Another detail worth remembering for safety-conscious investors is that while some munis are insured and thus rated triple-A, the safety of an insurance company is not equal to the full faith and credit of the United States government. That makes pre-re's preferable for those who want the greatest safety.

Protection from Inflation

PRUDENT INVESTORS HAVE ALWAYS SOUGHT protection from inflation, especially since the economic stagnation of the 1970s and early 1980s. Another concern has been the need to reduce risk by diversifying portfolios, allocating investments among stocks, fixed-income investments, and possibly other categories of assets. Unfortunately, these two goals—protection from inflation and diversifying assets—often seemed to clash.

Because of inflation, some investment theorists have maintained that stocks are safer than bonds. But with equities there is no guarantee that principal will be protected; a stock price can drop to zero. Since the late-1990s emergence of the instruments described below, however, there has been no need for the twin goals of inflation protection and asset diversification to clash for American investors.

TIPs and Series I Bonds

THE UNITED STATES TREASURY introduced inflation-indexed Treasuries, or TIPs, in January 1997 and Series I savings bonds in September 1998. Both pay interest that is exempt from state and local taxes, and federal taxes on Series I bonds can be deferred until redemption—up to thirty years. Several countries have offered inflation-protected bonds for decades, and now the United States does, too.

On both TIPs and Series I bonds the earnings rate is calculated by the Treasury from two separate rates: a fixed rate of return and a variable semiannual inflation rate, which is based on movements in the Consumer Price Index (CPI). Series I bonds are sold continuously, and for those issued between May 1 and November 1, 2001 the rate at issue was 5.92 percent, well above the 5.58 percent coupon on the regular long Treasury bond at that time. Various issues of TIPs are available in the secondary market.

Series I bonds offer several advantages over TIPs. Taxes on the earnings from Series I bonds can be deferred until sale or maturity. Also, if a Series I bond is used for qualifying educational expenses and the owner's income is within certain limits (see Chapter 8), the interest on the redeemed bond is not subject to federal income taxes. TIPs offer no such deferral or exclusion.

Bondholders who redeem their Series I securities within the first five years forfeit three months' worth of earnings. People who cash them in later than that receive the "inflated" full face value. In contrast, TIPs have far more price risk than Series I bonds, because TIPs are marketable securities with no price guaranteed until the government redeems them at maturity. A bondholder who wants out before they mature must sell them to someone else; it is not possible to redeem them back to the government.

Another advantage of Series I bonds is that they provide greater protection against deflation than TIPs. The interest credited on Series I securities can never go below zero, and the principal is always protected. The interest rate on TIPs can be negative, which will erode principal.

For many affluent investors, the main drawback of Series I bonds is that there is an annual purchase limit of $30,000 per Social Security number. Consequently, these bonds work best as part of a long-term investment strategy.

Series I bond order forms can be obtained from most banks and thrift institutions. Also, the government provides information about both Series I bonds and TIPs at www.publicdebt.treas. gov. It also offers purchase plans online at the same site through its Buy Direct program.

FIXED-INCOME INVESTMENTS have a place in most portfolios, both for diversification and to provide a predictable income stream to meet specific needs, such as college costs or living expenses for retirees. Many people automatically turn to municipal bonds for the fixed-income portion of their portfolios, but the three types of investments described above are likely to provide better returns on an after-tax equivalency basis.

CHAPTER 5

Hedging to Avoid
Capital Gains Tax

Protecting Appreciated Positions
and Getting Money out of Stock
without Paying Tax

INVESTORS WITH APPRECIATED STOCKS often want access to the cash value of their securities, but they hesitate to sell for two reasons. Selling could mean they would have to pay capital-gains taxes, and it would foreclose benefiting from future appreciation.

What many investors do not realize is that they can have it both ways by hedging. They can get money out of the holding without having to pay taxes and thus reducing the value of their portfolios. What is more, hedging can safeguard the unrealized gains in their stock—while maintaining some of the stock's upside potential.

Basic Hedging Strategies

THE SIMPLEST HEDGING STRATEGY is to buy a put option. That gives the investor the right to sell a stock at a given price for a certain length of time. An "at-the-money" put gives the investor the right to sell the stock at its current market price, thereby allowing the investor to put a floor under that price without selling the stock and, therefore, without limiting the upside potential. However, the cost of this comfortable position is high— 10 to 12 percent annually at present—and that makes an at-the-money put prohibitively expensive as a long-term hedge.

Another traditional technique aimed at protecting a long-term gain in a security is known as selling short against the box. In a short sale securities that have been borrowed are sold, generally in the expectation that the price will decline and the seller will be able to repay the loan with lower-priced shares. But in a short against the box, the investor borrows shares identical to those he already owns to protect a paper profit; the word "box" dates from the days when investors took delivery of stock certificates and kept them in a safe-deposit box. Selling stocks short against the box was limited but not halted by the Taxpayer Relief Act of 1997. However, this highly effective technique may still be used with debt securities. (See Chapter 14.)

Collars

IN CONTRAST TO THE STRATEGIES described above, this premier hedging technique remains fully available to investors with substantial assets. Collars—the purchase of put options and the simultaneous sale of call options with a strike price above the stock price—can safeguard unrealized gains in the stock. Calls are the opposite of puts. A call gives the buyer the right to purchase a given stock at a given price within a given time. The collar, in effect, establishes a minimum price or floor through the put and a cap above it through the call. Collars are often implemented using over-the-counter options, but you can also choose listed options, including so-called equity-flex options, which are exchange-traded options that allow the investor to custom-tailor most contract terms, including strike price, expiration, and exercise style. These listed options also offer some extra tax benefits under certain circumstances.

To be sure, collars must be structured carefully to avoid incurring gain. Section 1259 of the Internal Revenue Code sets out conditions in which a taxpayer will be treated as having constructively sold an "appreciated financial position"—that is, a position in which there would be a gain should it be sold, assigned, or otherwise terminated at its fair market value. To stay within this rule, a hedge, rather than simply assuring a gain, ought to retain some risk of loss or potential for profit. There is no specific guidance, either in law or in IRS regulations, as to how much risk (or upside) must be retained to avoid running afoul of the constructive-sale rule. The law permits the use of options provided they are not abusive, but it does not specify what is abusive.

So at Twenty-First Securities we look for guidance in what is known as the "Blue Book," a publication of the Congressional Joint Committee on Taxation. In the General Explanation of the Constructive Sale Rule, the Blue Book cites the example of a commonly used collar that has a put at 95 percent of the current market price and a call at 110 percent. That equates to a 15-point spread between the put and call strike prices, pointing toward the conclusion that a collar with a 5 percent loss potential and a 10 percent profit potential is not "abusive" and thus will not constitute a constructive sale.

Variable Forward Contracts

A related technique is the variable forward contract, which is a contract to sell a security in the future with the number of shares to be delivered at maturity varying with the underlying share price. The contract effectively has a collar embedded in it.

Both simple collars and variable forward contracts offer an appropriate risk/reward band, and both, upon disposition, produce capital gains or losses, rather than ordinary income or losses. There is, however, one possible cause for concern regarding variable forward contracts. Internal Revenue Service Field Service Advice (FSA) 200111011, which was released December 6, 2000, suggests that the use of a prepaid variable forward contract may create immediate taxation of the underlying shares.

In the Field Service Advice, which relates to the taxation of a debt instrument that has economic similarities to a prepaid variable forward contract, the IRS concluded that the issuer of the instrument was required to recognize a gain immediately upon entering into the transaction. The IRS contended that the benefits and burdens of ownership of the underlying shares had shifted to the purchasers of the debt instrument. It reached this conclusion even though the seller of the instrument was entitled to vote the underlying shares and receive dividends during the period the transaction was in effect and also had the right to substitute the collateral.

Although this analysis is troubling, the tax community does not consider it fatal to prepaid forward contracts. A Field Service Advice is essentially an informal letter that the IRS national office issues to an IRS examining agent. These letters are not considered binding on other taxpayers. Often, the analysis simply reflects the IRS's views on a particular transaction without considering competing positions, and accordingly, the letters tend to side with the IRS examining agent. Finally, the conclusions reached in this particular FSA are not well reasoned. Nevertheless, investors should be warned that prepaid variable forward contracts are not immune to attack: Specifically, the IRS may take the position that these transactions create an immediate taxable sale of the underlying shares. Therefore, a collar with actual options might well be preferable.

Zero-Cost Collars

Investors generally use two types of collars: zero-cost (or cashless) collars and income-producing collars. Zero-cost collars are the better choice for a bullish investor who expects the underlying stock to continue to gain in value, because they provide the greatest upside potential—$50 in the chart on the following page, compared with $20 for an income-producing collar (see page 61).

The reason for the name "zero-cost" is that the strike price of the call is set to generate exactly enough cash to pay for the put. But while the costless hedge allows the investor to maintain a potential for a profit in the position, it is probably inappropriate for those who wish to monetize—that is, borrow against the position without liquidating it—because it does not create income even though it entails borrowing costs. The cashless collar is really for people who are bullish on a position and who want to realize the added appreciation they expect but are nevertheless prudent enough to want to protect the downside.

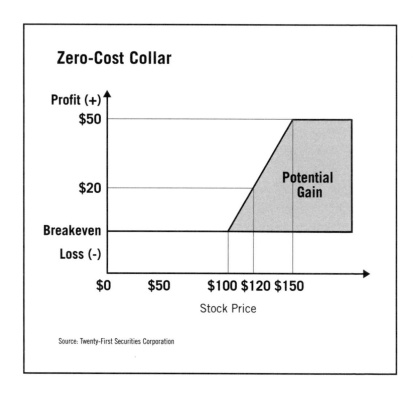

Source: Twenty-First Securities Corporation

Income-Producing Collars

Income-producing collars represent a more conservative approach than cashless collars for those who want to monetize their positions. They involve the purchase of a put and the sale of a call in which the strike price is relatively close to the current price of the underlying stock. The lower strike price generates more cash than is needed to pay for the put, but it also gives away more potential for profit in the collared stock. The choice of whether to go for the "bird in hand"—that is, the income-producing collar—or for the zero-cost collar depends on your view of the market and of the particular stock, as well as whether you have a current need for cash. If you are generally

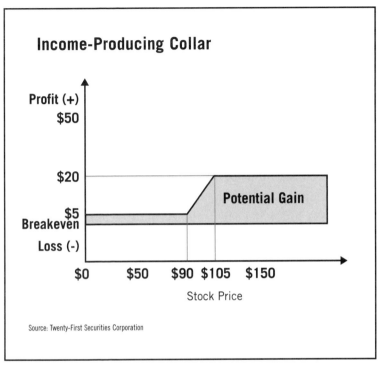

Source: Twenty-First Securities Corporation

optimistic about your stock and the market but are nevertheless prudent enough to want to protect your position, a cashless collar will fulfill your needs, but if you need to get cash out of a position while holding onto it, an income-producing collar will be the better choice.

Monetization

An investor with a substantial holding in a position can often monetize, or borrow against, the position to raise capital, rather than selling and recognizing a taxable capital gain. It is possible for investors to monetize their underlying positions with zero-cost collars to achieve this result. However, the combination of the two strategies is relatively expensive, because the zero-cost collar produces no income to pay the interest expense of monetization. You should therefore avoid this approach unless you have good reason to be extremely bullish about the future of the underlying security or the use of the borrowed funds. To avoid a maximum capital-gains tax of 20 percent while paying interest of 6 percent a year, an investor must make 30 percent from the underlying security or from the activity funded by the borrowed money.

The combination of monetization—that is, raising cash through a margin loan—and an income-producing collar represents a more appealing and cautious approach to managing low-basis stocks, because the cash earned by the income-producing collar can offset the interest expense of monetization.

For an example of this strategy, see the table in the sample transaction sheet on pages 64–65, which shows how an investor with 300,000 shares of Household International who borrowed 85 percent of the stock's value established protection against a drop in the stock's value of more than 10 percent and retained a 5 percent upside potential. To do this, the investor, who kept the dividend and voting rights, purchased a five-year, cash-settled put option and sold a five-year, cash-settled call option. The annual net cash flow of monetizing is a positive 0.15 percent. In other words, the investor was able to monetize a $17.7 million position and realize an annual net benefit of $26,550. Other investors can do the same, even though their positions will generally be significantly smaller.

Choosing the Best Strategy

ALTHOUGH THE TWO TYPES OF COLLARS presented above may be appropriate in many situations for hedging low-basis stock, they are not the only methods available. Indeed, there are many other types of collars and other ways, such as the variable forward contract, for example (discussed earlier in this chapter), to hedge or gain access to cash from a low-basis position.

All these strategies are complicated, and there could be changes in either tax law or SEC regulations, so investors should be certain of their situations before entering into a hedge. Nevertheless, it is possible to turn paper profits into cash without incurring immediate capital-gains tax liability. Hedging strategies are available, and informed investors will take advantage of them. Each strategy has different economic and tax implications, so you should choose what is most appropriate for your particular circumstances.

Hedging Pre-1984 Stock

WHEN LOOKING TO THE CIRCUMSTANCES in which you may want to hedge, even something as simple as when you bought a stock can be an important determinant as you decide which strategy to use. For stock purchased before 1984, when regulations known as the straddle rules went into effect, the best hedge is a swap with an embedded collar. The other two possibilities— options-based collars and prepaid variable forward contracts— produce less favorable tax consequences.

As discussed in earlier chapters, a swap is a contractual arrangement in which payments are referenced to a specified equity covering a notional amount. In this circumstance, the investor agrees to pay the swap dealer any profits over a specified price generated by the stock. The dealer, in turn, agrees to make payments to the investor equal to the amount that the shares are below a different specified price, thus creating a collar. For example, if the band is set at $90 to $105 and the share price climbs above $105, the investor pays the dealer the amount

Collar with Margin Loan: An Example

❑ **Objective:** A client seeks to protect an equity position with specific upside and downside exposure limits.

❑ **Transaction:** The client purchases a protective collar using equity options. Specifically, the client purchases a put option and sells a call option. The premium received from the sale of the call option offsets the premium due on the put option, with the balance going to the client.

❑ **Advantages:** The client is hedged below the strike price of the put option. The call premium is greater than the premium due on the put, thus creating a net credit from the option positions.

❑ **Disadvantages:** The client relinquishes price appreciation above the strike price of the call option.

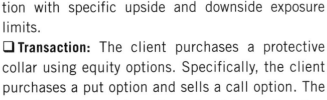

Expiration	Put % Strike	Put $ Strike	Call % Strike	Call $ Strike
5 years	90.0%	$53.10	105.0%	$61.95

% Target Borrow	$ Target Borrow	% Net Borrow	$ Net Borrow
85.0%	$50.15	69.1%	$40.75

Prices are indications only and there is no guarantee that the results set forth herein can be achieved. Any person or entity engaging in an options transaction must receive a current Options Disclosure Document prior to placing an order. Loan rates are determined from floating-rate benchmarks and may vary over the life of the transaction. However, loan rates have been assumed to be a known fixed rate for discussion purposes.

Date:	02/16/01
Underlying Name:	Household International
Underlying Symbol:	HI
Today's Price:	$59.00
Share Quantity:	300,000
Premium:	See chart below
Exercise Style:	European
Option Settlement:	Cash/physical
Collateral:	To be discussed
Dividends:	Client keeps

$ Net Premium Income / (Expense)	% Net Premium Income / (Expense)*	% Annual Net Income with Div Yield
$9.40	15.93%	4.47%

% Gross Annual Loan Rate	$ Gross Annual Loan Rate	% Effective Annual Loan Rate
-6.25%	-$2.55	-4.32%

Annual Net Benefit / (Cost) to Monetize:	0.15%

*Includes commission.

Source: Twenty-First Securities Corporation

the shares are above $105. If the stock price falls below $90, the dealer pays the investor the difference between $90 and the stock price. These payments are ordinary income. But if the investor closes the swap out early, the termination payments are taxed as capital. (See Chapters 1 and 2 for more discussion of swaps.)

Although all three hedging techniques mentioned above—swaps, prepaid variable forward contracts (discussed in detail earlier in this chapter), and options-based collars—can be effective financial tools, swaps generally produce the best after-tax results for transactions involving pre-1984 stock. Under certain circumstances, forward contracts and options can have unfortunate tax consequences. If the underlying stock increases in value, a forward produces a capital loss, which would be subject to capital-loss limitations. (Capital losses must be taken first against capital gains, and then up to $3,000 may be taken against ordinary income; any remaining losses are carried forward to future years.)

As noted previously, the tax treatment on swaps is more generous. The payments made according to the contract are treated as ordinary, although if a swap is terminated early, the results are treated as capital in nature. That means that with proper planning a swap investor ought to be able to recognize either a capital loss or an ordinary loss.

If the underlying stock declines in value, the investor could end the swap early, creating a long-term capital gain. If the underlying stock appreciates, the resulting loss is ordinary if the contract is not terminated early. That means it can be deducted against ordinary income and is not subject to the capital-loss limitations, so that the entire loss may be deductible in the current year instead of being carried forward for many years, as a large capital loss might.

On the other hand, if the stock increases, you earn more

long-term gains taxed at 20 percent, rather than ordinary income taxed at 38.6 percent, and by leaving the swap in place until termination, the money you lose on the hedge is deductible against ordinary income. That means that for every dollar rise in the stock price, there is almost 20 cents in tax savings. For example, if a hedged stock that is trading at $50 goes to $80, the investor will have a $30 gain taxed at 20 percent if the shares are sold and an offsetting $30 loss on the swap that can be taken against ordinary income that would have been taxed at 38.6 percent—a positive after-tax difference of $5.58.

To be sure, swaps have a possible drawback for some taxpayers. Because any loss is ordinary, it is a miscellaneous itemized deduction. Such deductions can be taken only to the extent that in total they exceed 2 percent of a taxpayer's adjusted gross income; the first 2 percent stays nondeductible. Thus, if a taxpayer already had enough other miscellaneous itemized deductions to exceed the 2 percent floor, all the swap losses would be deductible; if a taxpayer did not meet that threshold otherwise, then all or part of the swap losses might not be deductible.

Further, the value of itemized deductions is reduced by phaseouts for upper-income taxpayers. For those subject to the alternative minimum tax, the deduction is not allowed at all. Given these possible problems, you should consult your tax adviser to determine whether it is better to have an ordinary deduction subject to these limitations or to have a capital loss. You can manage the swap to produce either one, and you can make the choice after you know the results.

Only substantial investors are eligible to participate in swaps. Most dealers require that a swap have a minimum notional, or benchmark, value of $3 million. Further, only individuals who have gross balance sheet assets of at least $10 million qualify as swap participants.

If the investor wishes to monetize the position—that is, get money out of it—the best way is to borrow against the hedged stock position. Beware of prepaid variable forward contracts for this purpose, however, which by their nature automatically capture all carrying costs as capital losses rather than as interest expense. As a result, investors who use this tool may never be able to deduct the carrying charges.

Hedging Post-1983 Stock Using One-Instrument Collars

FOR STOCK ACQUIRED AFTER 1983, the best hedge involves an options-based collar that combines the put and the call into one instrument. The key difference between stocks acquired before 1984 and those acquired after 1983 is that post-1983 shares are subject to the straddle rules, so care must be taken to avoid problems when they are hedged with a collar. These rules have two significant repercussions, the first affecting all investors who hedge post-'83 stock with collars and the second affecting those who borrow as well as hedge.

Straddle Rules and Hedges

A straddle consists of a security and another position, where each reduces the risk of the other. If a position is deemed to be a straddle, none of the losses realized on any leg of the collar can be deducted until all positions are closed. In contrast, profits are taxable immediately as short-term capital gains at ordinary income rates of up to 38.6 percent. As a result, any future option transactions could create a whipsaw of phantom taxable profits.

For example, suppose that XYZ is selling at $100 a share. The investor constructs a three-year, zero-cost collar on the stock, buying puts struck at $90 for $14 and separately selling calls struck at $160 for $14. If the collar expires with the stock price between $90 and $160, the investor faces a tax of $5.40 (38.6 percent of $14) on each expired call, but the investor cannot currently deduct the "wasted" $14 cost of the puts. Although the investor protected the underlying position and created some potential for profit, he incurred an after-tax cost of more than $5 a share and realized no actual profits.

Suppose that instead of buying separate puts and calls, the investor hedges XYZ with a one-contract collar. Using this approach, the investor could create the same financial structure—in other words, effectively buying puts at $90 and selling calls at $160. But when a zero-cost collar is constructed using one option, the price of the option is zero. Thus, if the collar expires with the stock price anywhere between $90 and $160, the expiration would not create any taxable income or loss. The investor has created the same level of economic protection and potential for profit but has not incurred any additional tax burden.

Investors can create one-contract collars using any of the three basic collar strategies, whether working with actual options, swaps, or variable forward contracts. If the investor uses actual options, they must be traded over-the-counter, because listed puts and calls are (as of this writing) traded as separate entities, whereas over-the-counter options can combine puts and calls into one instrument. If the investor uses swaps or variable forward contracts, then the embedded put and call will also offset each other. Swaps could produce ordinary income, which would make them less tax-efficient than the other techniques.

Straddle Rules and Monetization

As noted previously in this chapter, investors with appreciated stock who wish to get money out of their positions without selling and incurring a capital gains tax may choose to monetize—that is, borrow against—their appreciated stock. Borrowing creates interest expense, and if that expense occurs in conjunction with a straddle, capitalization rules might apply.

Under the terms of the most recent *proposed* regulations, which reflect the government's recent rulings, if collared shares are the only collateral used for a loan, the interest must be capitalized. Because of the "direct-tracing" rule in the proposed regulations, if an investor has other liquid securities to post as collateral, it would still be possible to deduct the interest expense. For example, if an investor with $100 of hedged shares borrowed and reinvested in $100 of securities, leaving only these positions in the account, only half the interest expense would be currently deductible. The remaining 50 percent would have to be capitalized.

Investors can monetize with any of the three basic hedging strategies by borrowing against the hedged position. In certain cases, Federal Reserve rules limit investors' ability to monetize with options-based collars. For this reason, and through the force of general usage, many investors wishing to borrow rely on prepaid variable forward contracts. However, with this strategy, the nature of the contract automatically captures all carrying costs as capital losses rather than as interest expense. As a result, investors who use this tool may never be able to deduct the carrying charges. It can thus be argued that this approach is too expensive in terms of taxes.

If an investor employs a variable forward, it should not be

prepaid. Rather, a separate borrowing method should be used for the monetization, just as it should with a swap or one-contract option. Indeed, the only time a variable forward contract should be prepaid is when Federal Reserve rules or other regulations prevent the investor from using other strategies to monetize. If regulations do not force an investor who wishes to monetize into a prepaid variable forward contract, then either an options-based collar or a variable forward contract that is not prepaid will be a superior choice.

Hedging Restricted Holdings

OFTEN EXECUTIVES AND OTHER high-level employees receive compensation in stock that cannot be traded on the public securities markets for a period of time. Many investors are unaware that they can, nevertheless, hedge these restricted holdings, which, under Rule 144, cannot be sold into the public market for one year after acquisition. In fact, investors can hedge without stopping the clock for these purposes. Several of the basic hedging techniques—swaps, collars, and variable forward contracts—may be used for hedging new restricted positions. These hedges demand collateral, and although brokers generally refuse to accept such stock as collateral before the one-year holding period has passed, proper structuring can solve these problems.

Standardized listed options—that is, American-style options—are not viable for restricted stock because they can be exercised at any time. As a result, brokers cannot accept restricted stock as collateral for such options. However, European-style options, which can be exercised only on the expiration date, are viable. Investors can use OTC or exchange-traded E-flex options, on which terms can be set, to hedge restricted stock. Both allow the investor to choose European-style option settlement. By selling options that expire after the one-year holding period mandated by Rule 144, the investor can use the restricted stock as collateral.

Establishing "proper" collateral on swaps, OTC options, and variable forward contracts is a matter for negotiation between the two parties entering into the contract. Therefore, an investor may want to get competing quotes, just as she would when shopping for a car or a co-op.

Investors should also be aware that there is an active private market for selling restricted stock before its one-year holding period is up. The buyer assumes the restrictions of the original holder and thus will pay the market price minus a discount for the monies tied up and the shares' lack of liquidity. The price paid is based on how much time is left in the holding period and the buyer's ability to hedge the long shares. The mechanics are somewhat complicated to complete and can take up to two weeks. If you have such stock and want to sell it, the first place to turn to is your broker. Some brokers will handle the stock in a private transaction, while others may serve as a liaison for a specialized firm. So for holders of restricted stock, remember it is saleable, although at a discount, or alternatively it may be hedged without stopping the clock on the holding period mandated by the Securities and Exchange Commission.

Finally, investors should be aware that the volume limitations imposed by Rule 144 may curb the size of a transaction. Also, there have been rumblings from the staff of the SEC about limiting investors' ability to hedge restricted holdings; so before acting, investors should check whether there have been regulatory changes.

A Diversification Strategy of Last Resort

SOMETIMES COLLARS OR forward sales contracts are ineffective in a particular circumstance or are unavailable to a stockholder because the dealer cannot hedge itself, the stock is illiquid, or similar shares cannot be borrowed for a short sale. In such cases investors may wish to consider exchange funds. Although this strategy does not permit monetization and offers less protection against market risks for appreciated securities than a hedge would, it does make it possible to diversify holdings, and from a market standpoint that is generally safer than having all one's eggs in one basket. Further, this diversification is achieved without having to sell the securities and reinvest the proceeds; consequently, capital gains taxes continue to be postponed.

Exchange funds are partnerships in which all the investors contribute stock in exchange for limited partnership interests. Each investor's interest represents the proportionate share of the diversified portfolio created by all the contributed stocks. Investors who leave their shares in a properly organized fund for more than seven years will not incur a gain when they subsequently withdraw from the fund and receive securities. A properly organized exchange fund must have no more than 80 percent of its assets in liquid financial instruments, such as stocks traded on the Big Board or Nasdaq.

Although investors may enjoy the tax-free diversification inherent in exchange funds, there are also drawbacks. The first stems from the 80 percent limitation. Most funds comply with this limitation by borrowing 25 cents for every dollar's worth of stock their investors contribute. The borrowed money is usually used to purchase nonpublicly traded preferred stocks of real estate investment trusts (REITs), a move that exposes the fund

73

to additional investment risk. If the REIT went bankrupt, the investor would be down 25 percent.

A second hazard is the "deadwood" effect. Investors are likely to contribute stocks they do not want, so the funds could hold some weak securities. The seven-year holding period compounds both risks. Consequently, using exchange funds is recommended only if there is no viable hedging alternative.

For investors who have determined that an exchange fund is the only means of diversification available to them, here are some suggestions: First, seek a large and diversified fund with relatively low costs and a track record reflecting a high correlation with a target index, such as the Standard & Poor's 500 stock index. A high-tech stock, for example, may be rejected by these broad-based exchange funds, so the most difficult task may be finding a partnership. An investor with such a stock could seek a fund that replicates the Nasdaq 100.

WITH PROPER PLANNING it is possible to protect yourself from the vicissitudes of the market without selling your stock prematurely and incurring a capital-gains tax liability. If you are going to employ one of the hedges discussed in this chapter you must ask yourself these questions: (1) Do you want to lock in your profits and leave yourself the possibility to make more profit, or would you sell if taxes didn't exist? (2) Did you purchase the shares before or after January 1, 1984? (3) Do you want to pull money out of the position?

The answers to these questions will dictate which tool to use. Help can be found at an interactive decision tree at www.twenty-first.com/strategies.htm.

CHAPTER 6

The Quest for Tax Efficiency in Mutual Funds

IF BEAUTY IS ONLY SKIN DEEP, it is still deeper than some advertising claims. We are thinking specifically of the claims by a small but growing number of mutual funds that promote themselves as "tax-efficient" or "tax-managed."

The Law Requires Distributions— Taxes Result

MUTUAL FUNDS, ESPECIALLY IN tax-favored accounts to save for retirement or education expenses, have great strengths. The two classic arguments for investing in funds are diversification and professional management. And for proponents of the efficient-market theory, who believe that over time it is impossible to beat the market, there are index funds that replicate popular benchmarks like the Standard & Poor's 500 stock index. Few individual investors have the wherewithal to invest in all 500 S&P stocks on their own.

But for regular accounts that are not tax-deferred, mutual funds have a glaring weakness: They are not tax-efficient. The reason is that the nation's securities laws require funds to make annual distributions to their shareholders of the capital gains they recognize and the dividends they receive. In contrast, when a growth stock is owned directly, it can be a great tax shelter. Investors can own such a stock for years and owe no taxes on it until they choose to sell, thus recognizing their gains. But fund investors have no such control. If the fund distributes gains and dividends, shareholders must pay taxes accordingly, even if the distribution is reinvested in the fund.

"Over the past five years, taxes have effectively cost fund shareholders about 2.3 percentage points a year, about 10 percent of the return," *Business Week* reported in an article entitled "Mutual Funds: What's Wrong," on January 24, 2000.

To be sure, the annual tax liability is a problem only for the 35 percent of the $6 trillion in fund investments that are held in regular taxable accounts. According to the Investment Company Institute, the fund industry's trade organization, 65 percent of fund shares are held in tax-deferred accounts, such as retirement plans and annuities. The institute reported that funds distributed a record $345 billion in capital gains to shareholders in the year 2000, far surpassing the previous high of $238 billion set one year earlier. With more than one-third of fund holdings in regular taxable accounts, many fund industry leaders have become concerned about how to lessen the tax bite caused by these distributions.

The Exchange-Traded-Funds Alternative

For individual investors who are concerned about tax problems in connection with their fund holdings a clear alternative is exchange-traded funds, or ETFs. These funds are baskets of stocks that usually mimic an index, much as an index fund does, but that trade as a single stock would on the American Stock Exchange, rather than being sold directly like a traditional mutual fund. For example, both a traditional mutual fund, the Vanguard 500 Index Fund, and an exchange-traded fund, the Standard & Poor's Depositary Receipts (popularly known as Spiders for its initials, SPDRs), mimic the S&P 500 stock index. When index components are changed, as they are from time to time, managers of both the traditional index fund and the SPDRs must sell stocks that are dropped from the index, and both must make a distribution to shareholders.

If capital gains are realized from redemptions, the traditional mutual fund passes them on to shareholders, and those who have regular taxable accounts then face a tax liability. But ETFs manage redemptions differently. When people cash out of an ETF, the fund, rather than selling and realizing a gain, generally distributes a proportionate slice of the shares that would have been sold. In other words, the ETF makes a distribution in kind. As the tax laws work, this eliminates one level of tax. For tax efficiency, more funds should distribute in kind, especially U.S.-based hedge funds, virtually all of which involve taxable accounts.

Folios, Another Possibility

A relatively new tax-efficient alternative to traditional mutual funds is folio investing. This is a concept introduced by Steven Wallman, founder and chief executive of FOLIOfn and a former commissioner of the Securities and Exchange Commission. The folios are baskets of stocks that provide the diversification of funds, but investors own the stocks directly, thereby retaining the control needed for tax efficiency. Investors trade online (www.foliofn.com) and may buy either prepackaged folios, some of which are based on popular indices like the Dow Jones Industrial Average, modifying the folio's content if they like, or put together their own folios of up to fifty stocks each. Investors pay either a monthly fee of $29.95 or an annual fee of $295 to trade as much as they like in up to three folios, and for additional fees can trade more. In comparison with typical mutual fund fees, that means folios are generally appropriate only for investors with portfolios of $25,000 or more.

Explaining the tax efficiency of the system, Wallman said: "Our system tracks every stock purchase and sale and lets you choose one of eight different ways to determine which tax lots you want to sell for what kind of tax result you want. For example, you can set the system to find the sale that will minimize gain and maximize loss. If you qualify for capital-gains treatment and hold the stock long enough, you'll get long-term capital gains.[1] Furthermore, you can practice loss harvesting. Say you own Folio 30 [the Dow stocks] and the market has had a great year, but even so a handful of Dow stocks have skidded—you can sell them, which is something no one in a traditional index fund or ETF can do."

John Bogle's View

Not everyone in the traditional mutual fund industry is indifferent to the tax impact that portfolio managers' decisions have on shareholders. John C. Bogle, the former senior chairman of the Vanguard Group, calls taxes "the industry's black sheep." In his 1999 book, *Common Sense on Mutual Funds,* Bogle wrote, "Like a cousin who can't get her life together or an uncle who drinks too much, taxes are kept out of sight and out of mind." The shareholder suffers, he argues, "for it is the fund shareholder who pays the taxes on a mutual fund's income dividends and on any capital gains distributions generated by the fund's constant staccato of portfolio sales and—at least in the recent bounteous bull market—by the realization of enormous taxable capital gains. The dichotomy is that a portfolio manager's performance is measured and applauded on the basis of *pretax* return—never mind that the Internal Revenue Service confiscates a healthy share of it. Most portfolio managers simply don't spend much time agonizing over the tax consequences of their decisions."

Bogle's recommended alternative to this particular drunken uncle or negligent portfolio manager—not surprisingly, for he was the founder of the enormously successful Vanguard Index 500 fund—is to invest in index funds. He points out that index funds do not have the high portfolio turnover that actively managed funds often have, and it is turnover that leads the managed funds to incur taxable capital gains. Bogle cites persuasive statistics to support his argument. For the fifteen years ended June 30, 1998, an S&P 500 index fund provided an annual rate of return of 16.9 percent before taxes and 15.0 percent after taxes, well outpacing the average mutual fund's 13.6 percent before taxes and 10.8 percent after taxes.

"Tax-Efficient" Funds

OTHERS IN THE FUND INDUSTRY have agreed with Bogle's diagnosis of the industry's tax problem but not with his prescription for dealing with it. Having never given up on the idea that active management could produce winning results, some fund managers, although they are a small minority, have succeeded in outperforming the benchmarks, especially in the bear market of 2000 and 2001, when a number of actively managed funds lost less than the market indices. The professionals in this camp have concluded that the best approach to solving the tax problem is to manage funds in such a way as to minimize the tax liability that shareholders face.

The Ideal Fund: Where Failure Leads to Success

Ironically, a key aspect to future tax efficiency in a mutual fund is precisely what a manager would not try to achieve: big losses. A fund that is tax efficient as measured by the ratio of after-tax returns to pretax returns could nevertheless pose future tax problems to investors if its portfolio is chock-full of unrecognized capital gains. Should the manager recognize those gains, either for reasons pertaining to routine portfolio adjustments or because a severe down market has led shareholders to redeem holdings, so that he must raise cash, the gains will, of course, be passed on to shareholders.

That is precisely what happened to investors in August 2000 in two Warburg Pincus funds: Japan Small Company Fund, which paid out 55 percent of assets in the form of short-term gains taxable as regular income, and Japan Growth Fund, which paid out 20 percent of assets. The reason for the payouts was that the funds, after rising sharply in 1999—329 percent and 266 percent respectively—had much lower returns in 2000, leading to redemptions.

Even shareholders in one "tax-managed" fund found themselves owing big capital-gains taxes. The Standish Small Capitalization Tax-Sensitive Equity Fund, which had gained 285 percent since inception, made a 14.3 percent distribution to shareholders, also in August 2000. The fund's former investment team, led by Nicholas S. Battelle, considered the climb by some high-flying technology and biotechnology issues overdone and sold the holdings before reality set in. Battelle sold other winning stocks, including Human Genome Sciences and DoubleClick Inc., because they no longer fit the definition of small-cap stocks. Despite these recognized gains, the overall portfolio fell, as did most funds and market indices in 2000. *The New York Times* reported that if you had put $100,000 into the fund at the beginning of the year 2000, your portfolio's value would have lost $13,783 and you, nevertheless, would have owed $7,796 in taxes, ending the year with an effective net of $78,421.[2]

The Wall Street Journal quoted Battelle as having said that he was walking a tightrope in keeping the fund tax efficient, investments small, and holdings reasonably valued. "There's never a clear path through all that," he said.[3]

Conversely, if a fund's portfolio has a lot of capital losses, as many technology funds in particular had during the bear market of 2000 and 2001, the manager can use them to offset sales of winners that have met investment objectives, thereby avoiding passing on capital gains to shareholders. When a fund has losses, it does not pass them on to shareholders; rather, they offset gains once gains are recognized.

So in searching for an ideal tax-efficient fund, look for a fund that is sitting on big capital losses but that looks promising going forward. Perhaps you think a fund was overly battered during a bear market and is bound to rise when investor psychology stabilizes, or perhaps the fund has brought in a promising new manager.

Comparing Fund Performances

Incurring economic losses, of course, is not how the actively managed funds seek tax efficiency. Rather, they try to hold down portfolio turnover, deliver the highest-cost stock first when selling, and harvest losses to the extent they have them.

By using these techniques, have they succeeded? Or to pose the question in the vernacular: Can you teach a pig to sing? Well, some squeal more prettily than others.

Despite the admirable goal of defanging the tax bite, in practice neither the tax-managed funds offered by some of the leading fund families nor the index funds were terribly successful in the three years ended June 30, 2001, as the table on pages 84–85 indicates. Significantly, in the last twelve months of that period the S&P 500 stock index lost more than 17 percent of its value, and many fund returns were battered. That is why the results in the table differ so markedly from the fifteen-year results reported by Bogle for the period ended June 30, 1998.

The table is not intended to recommend any fund, nor is it by any means a comprehensive listing of funds—there are more than 7,000 in existence. Rather, it is a sampling of funds using data gathered from Morningstar Inc. Data for six of the tax-managed funds that Morningstar cited in an article entitled "Tax-Managed Funds Keep Uncle Sam at Bay" were gathered, along with comparable data from seven popular funds, including the Vanguard 500 Index fund, which is often used as the benchmark for measuring fund performance. Finally, two screens were run to find the top performers in the Morningstar categories that included most of the tax-managed funds—namely, large blend and domestic hybrid. From this study, the following observations may be made:

❑ **The fund with the greatest tax-efficiency ratio** (99.21) and the greatest average annual tax-adjusted return (34.44 percent), Smith Barney Aggressive Growth A, did not market itself as tax-managed. It should be noted, however, the fund had a potential capital gains exposure of 46 percent.

❑ **Another large-growth fund that did not market itself as tax-managed,** Janus Mercury, also had more impressive performance figures than any of the tax-managed funds—an average annual tax-adjusted return of 12.00 percent—and, because of past capital losses, it was sitting on a negative capital gains exposure of 29 percent.

❑ **Five tax-managed funds** (the J. P. Morgan fund modestly calls itself "tax-aware," not tax-managed) produced better tax-adjusted results than some of the more widely held mutual funds and lower tax-adjusted results than others. As a group, their tax-adjusted results were only a bit lower than their average pretax returns, so that their tax-efficiency ratios tended to be higher than other funds, but only the J. P. Morgan fund had a very low potential capital gains exposure.

❑ **Some popular funds** (notably Fidelity Contrafund and Oakmark I fund) that are not tax-managed have a significant disparity in pretax and tax-adjusted returns, making them far more attractive for tax-deferred accounts than for regular accounts.

Clearly, you cannot rely simply on a tax-managed label to protect yourself. You need to do much more research about a fund's performance and investing style—and compare the findings with those for other funds—before buying.

Furthermore, you need to know much more than is evident from the numbers alone. For example, that 29 percent negative capital gains exposure of Janus Mercury ought to give the fund a significant tax advantage going forward. But an even more important fact that does not show up in a statistical study is that the fund changed managers early in the year 2001. Before deciding whether to invest in a fund, look

Comparing 15 Funds before and after Taxes
Data for period ended June 30, 2001

Fund	Morningstar Category
Smith Barney Aggressive Growth A	Large Growth
Smith Barney Security & Growth	Domestic Hybrid
Janus Mercury	Large Growth
PIMCO Growth & Income Institutional	Large Blend
Federated Kaufmann K	Mid-Cap Growth
T. Rowe Price Tax-Efficient Balanced	Domestic Hybrid
Vanguard Tax-Managed Balanced	Domestic Hybrid
Fidelity Magellan	Large Blend
J. P. Morgan Tax-Aware U.S. Equity	Large Blend
Schwab 1000 Investments	Large Blend
Vanguard Tax-Managed Growth & Income	Large Blend
Vanguard 500 Index	Large Blend
Fidelity Contrafund	Large Growth
Oakmark I	Mid-Cap Value
Evergreen Tax Strategic Foundation A	Domestic Hybrid

Tax-managed funds are highlighted.
Source: Morningstar, Inc.

3-Year Average Pretax Return	3-Year Average Tax-Adjusted Return	% Rank in Category	Tax-Efficiency Ratio	Potential Capital Gains Exposure
34.72%	34.44%	1	99.21	46%
20.48	16.26	1	79.40	22
14.95	12.00	5	80.28	(29)
21.25	9.44	4	44.42	(11)
12.63	7.52	42	59.56	20
6.65	5.92	9	89.02	17
6.34	5.29	12	83.38	13
6.13	4.75	17	77.46	32
4.70	4.49	19	95.52	4
4.01	3.73	26	92.83	34
3.94	3.50	28	88.90	17
3.91	3.37	29	86.11	35
5.49	2.65	42	48.28	8
4.41	1.72	80	38.86	11
0.40	(0.25)	75	N.A.	6

into its history, current manager, and investment style.

Mark Hulbert, who writes the mutual fund column, "Strategies," in *The New York Times*, warned in October 2000 that investors should "avoid funds that have recently changed managers," because "new managers tend to clear the decks of stocks bought by the predecessors, generating abnormal levels of capital gains." Of course, Janus Mercury has losses to offset any gains that may be realized.

Scrutinizing the "Tax-Managed" Label

To dismiss the "tax-managed" label as an advertising claim may be too cynical. The difficulty may be, as the authors conclude in a seminal study published in September 1998 by Undiscovered Managers LLC of Dallas (www.undiscoveredmanagers.com/Mutual%20Funds%20&%20Taxes.pdf) that shifting a portfolio manager's focus to taxes can change his or her style to the detriment of fund performance.

The authors give three reasons for their study: (1) "to examine and 'debunk' three commonly held myths about taxes and mutual funds;" (2) to introduce the idea that each "fund has a tax life cycle that benefits some shareholders and reduces the after-tax returns of others;" and (3) to propose an approach to selecting funds for the best after-tax returns over time.[4]

> 1 **Debunking Myths.** The three myths and the authors' counterarguments can be summarized as follows:
> **Myth #1: Investors should select funds with low portfolio turnover because they will get better after-tax returns.**
> Yes, low turnover can mean recognizing fewer taxable gains, but "pretax returns are the single biggest determinant of great after-tax returns."

Myth #2: Index funds are almost always more tax efficient than actively managed funds. In fact, some actively managed funds have a higher tax-efficiency quotient than index funds. Furthermore, many index funds have large embedded gains averaging 36 percent of assets for index funds with $2 billion or more of assets under management. If a bear market were to lead many investors to redeem their fund holdings, the funds would have to sell some of their holdings. As a result, large taxable capital gains would be passed on to shareholders.

Myth #3: "Tax-efficient" funds give investors the best after-tax results. "Altering a manager's investment process in an attempt to be more tax-efficient could ... undercut the manager's ability to generate strong pretax returns." In fact, as the screen for funds' pretax and after-tax returns showed, several traditional funds delivered better after-tax returns.

Significantly, although the Undiscovered Managers study was written well before the market downturn of 2000 and early 2001, these conclusions held up when funds were screened after the end of the second quarter of 2001. Their bear-market warning was also borne out early in 2001, when some funds (notably Janus Venture Fund and Fidelity Investments' Select Software and Computer Services Fund) that had big holdings in the battered technology sector made sizable distributions to cover redemptions. That left investors facing a big capital gains tax liability, even though the net asset value of their holdings had tumbled.

2 **An Optimum Point in a Fund's Tax Life.** This point, the authors say, occurs when the fund's embedded gain is small and the fund is likely to experience a large inflow of new cash, conditions that occur most frequently with small, new mutual funds. Indeed, the early investors in such funds may be able to shift the tax liability to future investors.

3 Guidelines for Selecting Funds. The study gives investors four guidelines for selecting funds with the potential for the greatest after-tax returns: (1) Select only exceptional, experienced money managers with proven investment strategies; (2) invest in funds only at the optimum point in their tax life cycle; (3) select funds that coincidentally have tax-efficient returns; and (4) invest only in funds that use HIFO (highest cost in—first out) accounting. (This practice, by the way, ought to be routine for any fund, not only those that market themselves as tax-managed. See Chapter 10 for a discussion of delivering the highest-cost stock first.)

To follow these guidelines you clearly have to do some research before buying into funds. One possibility is to buy "clone funds." Putnam Investments, for example, has announced that it will clone successful funds (those with embedded gains of more than 15 percent) so that when new investors buy into a fund they will not wind up owing taxes on previous investors' capital gains. Still, a potential investor would want to study the particular fund and be sure it met his investment criteria, as well as being tax efficient, before buying.

How Funds Manage Taxes

WHAT ARE THE "TAX-MANAGED" FUNDS doing to live up to the moniker? The manager of one of the more successful funds, Terry E. Banet of J. P. Morgan's Tax Aware U.S. Equity Fund, has not distributed a capital gain since the fund began in December 1996. So far, she has succeeded in her goal of matching or surpassing the benchmark S&P 500 index, which relatively few managers have accomplished, and she has also held down the tax bite.

In an interview with *Investment Advisor*, Banet discussed the tax-management techniques she uses. They include loss harvesting (see Chapter 2 for a discussion of this vitally important practice), HIFO accounting, and relatively low portfolio turnover.[5] Further, to discourage redemptions, which can cause a fund to have to recognize gains, the fund charges a redemption fee of 1 percent during the first year, and shareholders who redeem more than $250,000 in fund shares may receive a distribution in kind—that is, twenty to thirty stocks—rather than cash, so that the fund does not have to sell shares.

An Accounting Strategy That May Be Risky

A TECHNIQUE THAT SOME FUNDS are using to scale back reportable capital gains is called "income equalization." The theory is that each redemption a shareholder makes from a fund during the year includes some amount of realized capital gains, and therefore some of the fund's gains should properly be allocated to the departing shareholder. Doing so will reduce taxable payouts to the remaining shareholders.

The problem, however, is determining what portion of the redemptions can be deducted. There are no clear IRS guidelines or rulings to indicate what might be proper equalization accounting. Consequently, should there be a future IRS audit of a fund that has used this accounting technique, and should the examiner conclude that the fund had severely underdistributed capital gains taxes and therefore owes substantial back taxes, current shareholders would suffer.

Warburg Pincus, a unit of the Credit Suisse Group, for example, said it had considered using equalization accounting to soften the blow to shareholders in its two Japanese funds with the big distributions in 2000. However, the firm said it decided not to do so because the IRS had not clarified which of various equalization methods was acceptable.

Funds are not required to disclose whether they use this accounting technique, but investors should be aware of it, and it is worth combing through a fund prospectus to see whether it might be discussed there.

Alternatives for Individual Investors

INDIVIDUAL INVESTORS WHO WANT to track an index or benefit from professional management and hold diversified accounts have three clear alternatives to investing in funds with their legally imposed tax inefficiencies.

One alternative is to invest in the relatively new exchange-traded funds. As discussed at the beginning of this chapter, these are baskets of stocks that are traded on the American Stock Exchange, such as the Standard & Poor's Depositary Receipts, or SPDRs, that mimic the S&P 500, just as the open-end Vanguard 500 Index fund does. Because ETFs distribute in kind—that is, distribute shares of stock rather than pass along capital gains in cash to shareholders—they are generally more tax efficient for investors than are regular mutual funds.

However, not even ETFs are immune from taxable distributions. Both iShares MSCI Canada Index Fund and iShares MSCI Sweden Index Fund paid capital gains distributions in cash in August 2000. The reason for the distributions, 23 percent and 18 percent respectively, was that some holdings had to be sold because of limits on the percentage of assets the funds can invest in a single stock. The Canada fund sold shares in Nortel Networks, while the Sweden fund pared its stake in the L. M. Ericsson Telephone Company.

The second alternative is the folios discussed above—baskets of stocks held directly that an investor can manage for tax efficiency. There are two possible drawbacks: The fees ($295 a year) make them generally appropriate only if you are investing at least $25,000, and they are for knowledgeable online investors, not for people who want personal professional advice.

The third alternative for people with sizable accounts who do want professional advice is to place their money with an individual money manager who makes direct investments, rather than investing through funds, and who can be more cognizant of an individual client's tax situation.

STRONG AFTER-TAX RETURNS are available in mutual funds, but it takes much more careful study to find them than simply buying a fund with "tax-efficient" in its name. The worst case for fund investors is when you are sitting on a paper loss in fund shares you own and, nevertheless, owe taxes on gains distributed on stocks that the portfolio manager purchased long before you bought into the fund. As the Undiscovered Managers' study said, the best predictor of strong after-tax returns is strong pre-tax returns. If you find a fund that satisfies that criterion, has a good manager, and has embedded losses that can be carried forward, you have an ideal fund investment.

PART 2

Tax-Advantaged Investment Opportunities

CHAPTER 7

Structuring
Your Retirement
Portfolio

O PEN ANY BOOK ON RETIREMENT planning—there are many—
and you are certain to find this advice: Take maximum advantage
of any tax-deferred pension plans that are available to you.

Typically, a number of reasons are given for tax-deferred
saving, among them:

❑ Much more money will accumulate when your account
compounds at a pretax rate of return than will accumulate
in a regular, taxable account.

❑ Your annual contributions to the plan will keep your current adjusted gross income down, which can be beneficial
in several ways at income tax time.

❑ Many employers match employees' contributions to retirement plans in whole or in part, and people who do not take
advantage of this match are leaving money on the table.

❑ With today's longevity, Americans are likely to need a sizable chunk of money for retirement. To accumulate

enough, most people will need a disciplined, long-term program of savings and investments.

One possible drawback is generally mentioned as well: If you withdraw money from a tax-deferred retirement plan before age 59½, you will owe taxes and, most likely, a 10 percent penalty.

Tax Deferral Is Advantageous Today, but Might It Lead to Future Problems?

THE ARGUMENTS IN FAVOR of tax-deferred retirement plans are undoubtedly true, but they do not tell the whole story. Much less is said about possible future problems. Significantly, you do not know at what rate your retirement distributions will be taxed. The assumption behind the laws authorizing the various retirement plans was that retirees were likely to be in a lower tax bracket than they had been in when they were working. So, the reasoning goes, although retirement distributions from the plan will be taxable, you will benefit by paying taxes at a lower rate than you would have paid had you invested the money in a regular taxable account and paid taxes all along the way. That assumption may or may not be true. A successful person might well be in a top tax bracket during retirement.

And who can say with certainty what tax rates will be ten, twenty, thirty, or forty years from now? If history is any guide, no one can. After federal income tax collection, which was authorized by the 16th Amendment, began in 1913, the top rate rose sharply during World War I from an initial 7 percent to a peak of 77 percent in 1918. As the accompanying chart shows, the top rate then tumbled during the 1920s to a low of 24 percent in 1929, only to resume its climb during the

Rates Are Headed Down, but the Course Could Change in the Future

Top marginal tax rates have fluctuated widely since the income tax was imposed. In deciding how to save for retirement, an important consideration is whether you are likely to be in a lower tax bracket or the same bracket as today—and since no one can know exactly what future tax law will be, it is important to review your retirement plans at least annually.

History of Top Federal Individual Income Tax Brackets

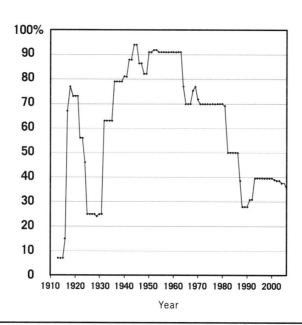

New Deal. It peaked at 94 percent at the end of World War II.

Rates did not come down substantially until 1964, when Congress passed the cut that had been championed by President John F. Kennedy, slashing the top rate to 70 percent from 91 percent. In 1982 the top rate fell to 50 percent after a half century above that level, and in 1988, as a legacy of President Ronald Reagan, to 28 percent. The 1990 budget agreement increased the top rate to 31 percent, and it subsequently climbed to 39.6 percent, the rate that was in effect until Congress passed the tax cuts urged by President George W. Bush, providing for a top rate of 38.6 percent effective July 1, 2001; 37.6 percent in 2004–2005; and 35 percent in 2006. But where will they go next? A lot could depend on whether the country elects an equivalent of Steve Forbes or Ralph Nader or someone in between.

Any change in future rates will affect distributions from tax-deferred accounts, because those distributions are taxed as ordinary income. Even if the growth of the account is largely attributable to capital gains, retirement distributions do not get the same favorable tax treatment that capital gains get in regular accounts.

Despite all the information that is available today about retirement planning, surprisingly little is said about how to structure a portfolio inside a tax-deferred retirement plan, and knowing that can be crucial to your long-term success as an investor. Congress has authorized a variety of tax-deferred retirement plans known as "qualified plans," as well as Individual Retirement Accounts, or IRAs. It is important to know not only for which plans you are eligible but also how to structure your retirement portfolio to maximize the tax advantages while avoiding the pitfalls and how the investments in the retirement plan fit into your overall financial plan or asset allocation model. We will address those points in this chapter.

Tax-Deferred Plans for Employees

Defined-Benefit Plans

Traditional defined-benefit plans have lost ground in recent years as defined-contribution plans have gained. Under a typical defined-benefit plan, when an employee retires, she receives a lifelong pension. The amount is based on the compensation she received, either for her entire years of service or more often for an average based on her last few years, times a factor specified in the plan and her length of service to the company. Investment decisions, which affect the overall plan's assets, are the plan administrator's responsibility, not the employee's. Although some plans index retirement distributions to inflation, most do not.

Defined-Contribution Plans

Defined-contribution plans give employees far more control over how much to save for retirement and offer a menu of investment options, often including a wide variety of stock and bond mutual funds and a guaranteed investment contract (GIC), a conservative fixed-rate, fixed-maturity issue that promises no loss of principal. The plans include 401(k) plans for employees of corporations, 403(b) annuities for employees of nonprofit organizations and schools, and 457 plans for government employees. Each plan is named after the section of the Internal Revenue Code that authorizes it.

A 401(k) plan is a qualified plan that allows participants to elect to contribute a specified portion of pretax compensation (limited to $10,500 in 2001) to the plan. Under the 2001 tax law, the limit is to rise annually, reaching $15,000 by 2006, and

$20,000 for people age fifty and older. The limit will be subject to indexing thereafter. Both the money contributed and the plan's earnings accumulate tax-free until they are distributed during retirement, and then distributions will be taxable. If a working person makes a premature withdrawal, it will be subject to income taxes and a 10 percent penalty. However, many plans permit participants to take out loans against their retirement savings, and that does not have any adverse tax consequences.

Some plans also permit employees to make additional contributions from after-tax compensation; those contributions are nontaxable when withdrawn.

Tax-Deferred Plans for the Self-Employed

Keogh Plans

Self-employed taxpayers, including employed people who also have self-employment income from a sideline business or director's fees, may save for retirement through what are popularly known as Keogh plans, after the Brooklyn congressman who introduced the legislation authorizing them. There are defined-benefit Keoghs and two forms of defined-contribution Keoghs: money-purchase plans and profit-sharing plans. If your self-employment income is from a business in which you have employees, the employees generally must be included in the Keogh plan.

The maximum annual tax-deductible contribution for a money-purchase Keogh plan is the lesser of $30,000 or 25 percent of net self-employment income up to $160,000. (Net self-employment income is self-employment income reduced by 50 percent of any self-employment tax liability and by the Keogh contribution itself.) The limit for profit-sharing Keogh plans is

15 percent. Greater savings are possible through the defined-benefit Keogh, especially for older people. A senior executive who serves on the boards of a couple of other companies, for example, might set up a defined-benefit Keogh plan for his director's income, which legally is self-employment income, and be able to put a substantial portion of it into the plan, where it can grow on a tax-deferred basis.

Simplified Employee Pensions, or SEPs

An alternative for self-employed taxpayers is a simplified employee pension, or SEP, which is also available to small employers. It is similar to an IRA but allows up to 15 percent of net self-employed compensation to be contributed, subject to some dollar limitations in the case of an unincorporated individual. As its name implies, it is simpler to set up and administer than a Keogh. Generally, you can simply fill out a one- or two-page form provided by a bank or brokerage that prepackages the plans. However, people who want to sock away as much as possible will find a Keogh more advantageous.

Tax-Deferred Plans Available to Anyone

Deductible IRAs

The majority of taxpayers can still contribute up to $2,000 apiece in a traditional, deductible IRA—and, thanks to the 2001 tax law, that limit is to rise gradually to $5,000 by 2008; for 2002–2003, it is $3,000. A catch-up provision allows people age fifty and older to contribute $3,500 a year in 2002 and 2003, rising gradually to $6,000 in 2008. Even people covered by an employer-sponsored pension plan may take the annual deduction if their income (for 2001) is below $53,000 for a couple filing jointly or $33,000 for a single person. The contribution limits are phased out for income of up to $63,000 for a couple and $43,000 for a single person.

As with a 401(k) plan, the contributions and earnings are not taxed until withdrawn. Similarly, withdrawals before age 59½ are generally subject to a 10 percent early withdrawal penalty, in addition to the regular income tax. The 10 percent penalty does not apply to distributions of up to $10,000 made after December 31, 1997, for first-time home purchases or for qualified higher education expenses for taxpayers, their children, or their grandchildren. Nor does it apply to distributions used for medical expenses in excess of 7.5 percent of the taxpayer's adjusted gross income.

Spousal IRAs

An individual who is not covered by a qualified retirement plan is no longer barred from making a deductible $2,000 IRA contribution simply because his or her spouse is covered, provided the couple's adjusted gross income is below $150,000, with a phaseout to $160,000. Even a nonworking spouse is allowed a spousal IRA.

Rollover IRAs

People who change jobs or quit working often have the option of rolling over all or part of their account balances in their former employer's retirement plans into IRAs. By taking advantage of this option, many people have much larger IRAs than would have accumulated from annual contributions of $2,000. For example, say a fifty-five-year-old executive decides to take early retirement and open his own business. He may roll his corporate pension into an IRA, so that the tax-deferred growth will continue as long as possible, and live on the income from the business he is establishing. If it is necessary to supplement that income with money from savings, it is better to take money first from regular taxable accounts rather than from tax-deferred plans, especially since he is below age 59½.

Nondeductible IRAs

People who are not eligible for a deductible IRA may still put money into a traditional nondeductible IRA. The rise in IRA contribution limits authorized by the 2001 tax law is effective for these IRAs, too. Although the contribution is not deducted from taxable income, the earnings on the contribution are not taxed until they are withdrawn. (For those who are eligible, a Roth IRA, which promises tax-free distributions, is better than a nondeductible IRA. See the discussion on the following page.)

Distribution Rules

FOR BOTH QUALIFIED RETIREMENT PLANS and deductible and nondeductible IRAs, account holders are legally required to begin taking distributions by April 1 of the year following the year in which they reach age 70½. Under IRS regulations announced in January 2001, a person aged 70½ has a life expectancy of 26.2 years. The applicable life expectancy can be lengthened if a younger person is named as the beneficiary of the IRA, and that will enable the account holder to take smaller distributions if he wishes. The money distributed will be subject to income taxes.

Withdrawals may be made by either the term-certain method (for a set number of years not to exceed the life expectancy) or the recalculation method, under which the account holder's life expectancy is recalculated every year to ensure that a person who takes minimum annual distributions will never run out of money.

Roth IRAs

The Roth IRA, which is still relatively new, is funded solely with after-tax (that is, nondeductible) contributions, but the earnings in the account accumulate tax-free, and when it is time to take distributions from the account, provided the money has been in the account for five years, the distributions are tax-free.

However, income limitations bar affluent people from taking advantage of Roth IRAs. The limitations begin at $150,000 for married taxpayers filing jointly and phase out at $160,000 and begin at $95,000 for single taxpayers and phase out at $110,000. Contributions are coordinated with any deductible IRA contributions that a taxpayer may make, and contributions of up to the maximum allowed for each year may be made to either type or to a combination of the two.

The distribution rules for Roth IRAs are much more taxpayer friendly than the rules for other retirement plans and IRAs. No distributions are required when the account holder reaches age 70½, and he may even continue to make contributions to the account.

Roth distributions made at least five years after the first taxable year in which the taxpayer contributed to a Roth IRA are not taxable, provided that any one of the following conditions is met:

1 the account holder is at least age 59½;
2 the distribution is because of disability;
3 the distribution is for a qualified first-home purchase; or
4 the distribution is to the account holder's estate or beneficiary.

By naming a child or grandchild the beneficiary of a Roth and not taking distributions oneself, an account holder can leave a stream of tax-free income to an heir.

Distributions of account earnings for other reasons are subject to the additional 10 percent early withdrawal tax, but annual contributions may be withdrawn without penalty. Distributions of account earnings for educational and medical expenses are taxable but are not subject to the 10 percent early withdrawal tax.

Converting to a Roth IRA

People whose adjusted gross income is below $100,000 may convert all or part of an existing IRA to a Roth IRA, but they must pay income tax on the amount that comes out of the regular IRA. Therefore, unless an account holder has other money with which to pay the taxes, it becomes a judgment call (or more properly a project for special software) to determine whether the future prospect of tax-free income more than offsets the shrunken size of the account due to taxes. As a rule, the longer the Roth has to grow, the greater the likelihood that the conversion will prove beneficial.

Comparing Returns of Tax-Deferred vs. After-Tax Accounts

CLEARLY, THERE ARE CURRENT tax advantages if you can defer income. The question is whether the hoped-for advantages will also be there during the retirement years. The answer: probably so, if the account is held long-term, but even then, not necessarily so.

The chart on page 108 compares growth of a $2,000 annual contribution to a deductible IRA with contributions to regular taxable accounts made from age forty until age sixty-five. A taxpayer in the top bracket (the number 36.6 percent appearing in the table represents a blended rate, inasmuch as the actual numbers have ranged from 31 percent in 1992 to 39.6 percent in recent years and are scheduled to fall to 35 percent in 2006) contributes $1,268 a year (the amount remaining after paying taxes on $2,000), while a middle-income taxpayer (a blended rate of 26.5 percent was used) contributes $1,470. The IRA grows at 8 percent a year, while the regular accounts grow at 5.072 percent (that is, 8 percent after taxes at 36.6 percent) and 5.88 percent (8 percent after taxes at 26.5 percent) respectively.

The account holders, although they retire at age sixty-five and do not continue contributing to their accounts, choose not to receive distributions until age 70½, when they are legally required to do so.

The difference in the account balances is dramatic: $234,959 in the tax-deferred IRA; $113,684 in the regular account for the middle-income taxpayer; and $83,871 in the regular account for the top-bracket taxpayer. Calculating the first year's IRA distribution based on the official life expectancy of 26.2 years, the top-bracket taxpayer would receive

$5,685.64 after taxes, compared with $3,201.18 from the regular account, assuming a withdrawal of a comparable proportion. The figures for the middle-income taxpayer would be $6,591.39 from the IRA after taxes and $4,339.09 from the regular account. But that is not the end of the story.

Suppose the middle-income taxpayer could sock away $2,000 a year in a Roth IRA, while paying an additional $721.09 in annual income tax on it, since Roth contributions are after-tax. His account would grow to that same $234,959, and his annual distributions would be $8,967.88, the hands-down winner.

Or suppose tax rates rise. Considering how they have seesawed historically, the current law cutting taxes should not be taken as a guarantee of where rates will be in thirty years. As the illustration on page 109 shows, at 50 percent, a taxpayer would have an after-tax first-year minimum distribution of $4,483.94 on the IRA, and at 70 percent, the distribution would be $2,690.36, meaning he would have been better off in a regular account. Granted, 70 percent may seem far-fetched, but it is not impossible.

Or, suppose a top-bracket taxpayer had put that same $1,268 into a regular account annually and all the portfolio growth had come from capital gains, rather than from dividends and interest. If she began comparable withdrawals at age 70½, she would be able to take out $4,548.51 a year after paying capital gains taxes at 20 percent, or about $1,000 a year less than she would be able to take out of her tax-deferred IRA.

An important consideration is time. These are long-term examples, which are appropriate for retirement investing, but in fact many people wait until they are within a few years of retirement to do serious planning and investing. If the accounts have only five or ten years to compound, the first-year distributions from taxable and tax-deferred accounts are much closer to each other.

Comparing First-Year Distributions at Age 70

Distributions from the tax-deferred account are taxable. Even so, minimum distributions, based on a 26.2-year life expectancy at age 70½ for a person who began putting away $2,000 a year at 8 percent at age 40 and did so until age 65, will be greater than if the person had saved $2,000 a year after taxes and the growth had been after taxes. That would still be true even if the retiree's tax bracket rose to 50 percent. If it went to 70 percent, he would be better off with a regular account.

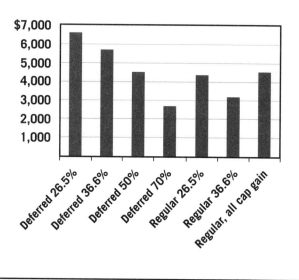

If all these numbers and future scenarios are beginning to seem confusing, yes, they are, and there are no guarantees about the future, in terms of account performance, tax rates, life expectancy, or inflation. But what is nearly certain is that anyone

Tax-Deferred Compounding Raises Balances

The graph shows how $2,000 would grow at 8 percent a year when contributed to a tax-deferred account, from age 40 through 65, and left in the account until age 70, compared with equivalent after-tax contributions and after-tax growth for investors in the top tax bracket (using a blended rate of 36.6 percent) and a middle-class tax bracket (using a blended rate of 26.5 percent).

Tax-Deferred Compounding

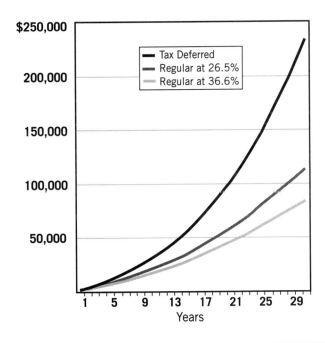

who retires will need money to live on, and probably much more money than Social Security will provide. And for many Americans, the discipline of saving through tax-deferred retirement accounts—and the psychology of doing so—are more important considerations than trying to figure out years in advance whether the tax advantage will prove to be as great as it is supposed to be. If you have your employer put part of your salary into a 401(k) or a 403(b) account, then if you are like most people, you will be inclined to leave it there. But most people find it far harder to save money from their paychecks. And if your employer matches your contributions, even partially, it would be foolish not to take advantage of that match. Say you put $11,000 into a 401(k) in 2002, and your employer puts in $5,500. Where else can you count on an immediate 50 percent return?

Structuring a Portfolio

LET'S SAY YOU ARE GOING TO MAKE tax-deferred retirement investments, because it is a disciplined way to save for retirement, because you want to take advantage of an employer match, because you need the current tax advantages—or all three. How do you invest the portfolio?

First, remember that the concept of capital gains versus capital losses does not apply to tax-deferred retirement accounts, and this gives rise to two key tax differences between them and regular accounts: (1) All distributions from a tax-deferred account are taxed as ordinary income, even if part of the money in the account came from capital gains, and (2) You cannot deduct losses that occur inside the account. Because the money was never taxed in the first place, no tax consequence arises if it is lost.

The implication for investors is that a tax-deferred retirement account is not the place for speculative, aggressive growth holdings. If you make a bad bet, there is no way to harvest your loss. If you make a good bet, you'll eventually be taxed at your regular marginal rate, not at a favorable capital gains rate.

Your Asset Allocation Model

If you are an affluent investor with both taxable and tax-deferred accounts, consider your entire investment portfolio when deciding which investments to allocate to tax-deferred retirement accounts and which to your regular accounts. Say you want 20 percent of your entire investment portfolio in growth stocks, 50 percent in blue chips, 25 percent in bonds, and 5 percent in cash equivalents. If 25 percent of your holdings are in your tax-deferred account, you are in an ideal position to use it for your bond holdings. If your tax-deferred account comprises 50 percent of your holdings, you could put your bonds and half your blue chips in it. Your riskier growth stocks should be in taxable accounts where you can either harvest your capital losses, using them to offset capital gains, or realize long-term gains if the investment is successful.

Mutual Fund Holdings

Because of the tax inefficiencies inherent in mutual funds (see Chapter 6), the tax-deferred account is an ideal place for certain fund holdings, provided they are not too aggressive. Funds are required to pass dividends and recognized capital gains on to shareholders every year, and if the funds are held in regular accounts shareholders are liable for taxes on them annually, even if the distributions are reinvested in fund shares. But the tax liability can be postponed if the funds are held in a tax-deferred account. For example, suppose you own half a dozen favorite stocks directly and also own shares in a mutual fund for diversity. The stocks could go in your regular account and the fund in the 401(k), which is also a good place for zero-coupon bonds for which taxes on imputed interest would otherwise be due annually.

But suppose you are a middle-class investor whose only investment portfolio is the 401(k). You cannot afford to be a gunslinger. Remember to protect the downside. If you choose an aggressive growth fund that loses 50 percent in one year, you will then have to make 100 percent just to get back to where you started. That, by the way, is why the examples above are based on an 8 percent return. There is a reasonable likelihood that a balance of funds invested in bonds and blue-chip stocks can achieve an 8 percent return. It is not reasonable over the long term to expect 20 or 30 percent returns. Many investors who aimed for such returns based on the stock market's performance of the late 1990s found their portfolios battered in 2000 and early 2001.

THE REASONS GIVEN AT THE BEGINNING of this chapter for taking advantage of tax-deferred retirement plans are valid at present. But planning for an event—retirement—that is five, ten, twenty, or thirty years in the future is shooting at a moving target. You should review and, if necessary, revise your retirement plan at least annually. If tax rates rise or your personal situation changes drastically, it will be important to revisit your plan. In any event, a tax-deferred account is a place for steady, conservative growth, not for risky holdings.

CHAPTER 8

Savvy Ways to
Save for College

O NE PLACE THE TAX CODE does not discourage investing is in saving for college—far from it. Whether in response to voters who are concerned about their children's futures or in recognition that an educated populace is in the national interest or both, Congress has authorized an almost bewildering array of tax incentives to put away money for education, and the 2001 tax act enhanced the tax breaks. The problem for parents and grandparents is a welcome one: how to choose the plan and the investments that will ensure the money is in place to pay for the kids' schooling and offer the greatest tax savings. What follows, we hope, will help you solve that problem.

Matching Assets and Liabilities

IF A SUCCESSFUL INVESTMENT is one that achieves the investor's goal, then success is assured for people who save for college by purchasing the CollegeSure® CD offered by the College Savings

Bank, in Princeton, New Jersey (www.collegesavingsbank. com). This is a certificate of deposit indexed to college costs that thus matches the amount needed to meet future tuition, fees, room, and board. To be sure, the rate of return on the CD is not known, but if you have the wherewithal to make the initial investment, you can match the asset (the CD) and the liability (college costs) and be sure that your child or grandchild's education will be funded. It's the best kind of financial engineering.

A stock portfolio or mutual fund in the best of times could offer a far more impressive rate of return, but, of course, there can be no assurance that we will have the best of times. The financial markets could go into a tailspin. So if you can choose an investment that will pay your children's college tuition no matter the cost, do you really care if, when all is said and done, it pays 3 percent or 12 percent?

What's more, savers in any state can realize significant tax advantages by investing in the CollegeSure® CD through qualified state tuition programs (discussed below) offered by Arizona (http//arizona.collegesavings.com) and Montana (http// montana.collegesavings.com). CDs of up to $100,000 are federally insured, and Montana's program material says, "A child with two parents and four grandparents can obtain up to $600,000 in FDIC insurance with properly structured accounts." People can call the College Savings Bank's toll-free telephone number, 1-800-888-2723, for assistance in structuring accounts for maximum FDIC coverage.

Less affluent families, however, simply may not have the assets or cash flow needed to buy the CDs. The College Savings Bank in June 2001 listed the cost of a public college as $9,635 a year, a private college as $24,088 a year, and an Ivy League college as $33,723 a year. Using a calculator on the bank's Web site to determine how much would be needed to pay for a four-year, private education for a child who is now three years old brought this answer: "Based on your child attending college in 2015–2018, if you were to prepay a four-year private college education today, you would need to deposit $99,955.30 to cover the projected future cost of $228,428.61. Or you could make annual deposits of $9,293.64, quarterly deposits of $2,261.60, or monthly deposits of $749.26."

Buying Savings Bonds

SAVINGS BONDS MAY BE ESPECIALLY appealing to less affluent families who are saving for college. The inflation-protected Series I bonds issued between May 1, 2001, and November 1, 2001, were yielding 5.92 percent at issue. At that rate, an up-front investment of $100,000 would grow to $223,713 in fifteen years, or about $5,000 less than nearly the same amount invested in the CollegeSure® CD. However, an I bond's composite earnings rate (which the Treasury calculates by using a formula that includes both a fixed rate and an inflation rate) changes every six months after its issue date, so if rates rise over the years, the return could surpass that of the CD.

A disadvantage of the savings bonds is that the inflation protection is linked to the consumer price index (CPI), not directly to college costs. The College Board said in a report issued in October 2000 that college costs had escalated twice as much and sometimes three times as much as the CPI since 1980. But an important benefit of the savings bonds is that interest on qualified Series EE bonds issued after 1989 or on Series I bonds is *not taxed* when the bonds are used for qualified education expenses for the bond's owner, spouse, or dependent, provided the taxpayer's adjusted gross income is

115

For College Savings, Tax Advantages Help

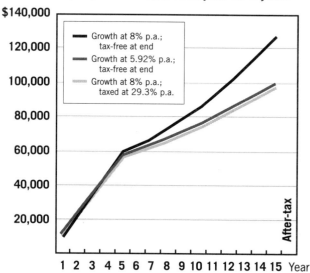

$10,000 invested each year for 5 years

Legend:
- Growth at 8% p.a.; tax-free at end
- Growth at 5.92% p.a.; tax-free at end
- Growth at 8% p.a.; taxed at 29.3% p.a.

Y-axis: $140,000, 120,000, 100,000, 80,000, 60,000, 40,000, 20,000 (After-tax)

X-axis: 1 2 3 4 5 6 7 8 9 10 11 12 13 14 15 Year

This graph compares three ways to invest $10,000 a year for five years beginning when a child is three and leaving the money to grow until the child enters college. If the money goes into a Section 529 program and earns 8 percent, it will be worth $126,656 when the child is ready for college, or 30.5 percent more than if it went into a regular taxable account where half the growth comes from interest and dividends and half from capital gains. By comparison, if the money were put into Series I savings bonds, based on the current yield of 5.92 percent, it would grow to $100,033.

Source: Twenty-First Securities Corporation

below $54,100, phasing out at $69,100 for single filers, or $81,100, phasing out at $111,100 for joint returns. The bond's owner must have been at least twenty-four years old at the time the bond was issued.

Following is a discussion of some of the other tax-favored strategies available for saving for college. As the accompanying chart shows, taxes can make a significant difference in how much will be available at enrollment time. If parents of a three-year-old invested $10,000 a year for five years in a regular account that yielded 8 percent a year and paid taxes at a blended rate of 29.3 percent (that's half at the long-term capital gains rate of 20 percent and half at their regular income tax rate of 38.6 percent), they would have $97,054 when their child entered college. If the money were put into a qualified state tuition program that also yielded 8 percent, when it was withdrawn to pay for college, the total would be $126,656—that is, $29,602 more on their $50,000 investment. (For comparison, using the Series I's 5.92 percent yield, the investment would grow to $100,033, and whether it was taxable or tax-free would depend on income level.)

Participating in Qualified State Tuition Programs

QUALIFIED STATE TUITION PROGRAMS, often called Section 529 programs after the section of the Internal Revenue Code that authorizes them, are offered by more than forty states, and all of the states except Georgia that do not yet offer them are planning to do so, according to SavingForCollege.com, an authoritative Internet site operated by Joseph F. Hurley, CPA.

Section 529 programs include both college savings plans and prepaid tuition plans—some states offer both—and the investment choices that are available range from the conservative to the speculative. Only Montana and Arizona offer the CollegeSure® CD; Arizona also offers a wide variety of other investment choices, while Montana offers only the CD.

Tax Benefits of the Programs

Among the plans' tax benefits are the following:

❑ **Tax-free withdrawals for college costs.** These plans have become even better, effective in 2002, thanks to the 2001 tax law. As in a Roth IRA, after-tax money is put into the Section 529 accounts, and the earnings are free from federal income taxes when the money is distributed to pay college expenses.

❑ **Deductions in many states.** Many states offer tax deferral on the earnings (in line with the previous federal law—and perhaps some will pass legislation to parallel the 2001 federal law making the earnings tax-free) and/or a deduction for contributions to the account. New York, for example, which sponsors a highly regarded plan (www.nysaves. com) administered by TIAA-CREF, allows state residents to deduct up to $5,000 a year per person for contributions to the plan. For a middle- or upper-income couple contributing $10,000, that amounts to tax savings of nearly $700. Montana allows its state residents to deduct up to $3,000 a year.

❑ **Reduction of taxable estates.** Section 529 plans, while only a few years old, have already won favor among affluent grandparents as a way to reduce taxable estates quickly. Typically, grandparents who help pay for their grandchildren's education costs do so by making annual gifts of

up to $10,000 per grandchild, or $20,000 if both a grand-
mother and grandfather make a gift (to as many grandchildren as they want), because an individual gift of up to
$10,000 has no gift- or estate-tax consequences. But there
is a special provision for Section 529 programs: A contributor can put in up to $50,000 in one year and elect to
take the annual exclusion ratably over a five-year period.
Thus, a married couple could put $100,000 into a plan,
which might well earn enough to pay for a four-year education at a private college. A couple with a half-dozen
grandchildren, say, could get $600,000 out of their taxable
estates and have the satisfaction of knowing their grandchildren's No. 1 financial need would be met.

❑ **No phaseouts.** Section 529 programs impose no income
limits for contributors, as do education IRAs and certain
other education benefits, including the Hope Scholarship
and Lifetime Learning credits (see the table on pages
124–127 for more information about these latter benefits).
As a result, the 529 program is especially well suited for
affluent investors who, in effect, are barred from other tax-
advantaged ways to save for their children's college costs,
Sidney Kess and Lee Slavutin wrote in a recent article for
CCH Inc.[1] "College savings plans will be most attractive
when the contributor is in a high income tax bracket and
invests conservatively, the state's plan offers state income
tax benefits (deductions for contributions or exemptions for
earnings), and the plan is started early," they said.

Investment Choices within the Programs

Among the options offered by many plans are such conservative
choices as bond funds or balanced funds that blend stock and

bond funds. Another way to invest conservatively is to allocate part of the holdings to bond funds and part to blue-chip stocks or a fund that mimics the S&P 500 stock index, and fortunately, many fund choices are available in Section 529 plans. Among the plan administrators for various states are TIAA-CREF, Fidelity, T. Rowe Price, Alliance Capital, Merrill Lynch, Salomon Smith Barney, and in some cases the states themselves. Some of the managers aim for heftier returns than others.

Some states, like Arizona, offer a wide-ranging menu of investments—although the experience of investors in Arizona's technology fund, which began on September 1, 2000, and tumbled 48.2 percent by year-end,[2] shows why we favor the CollegeSure® CD for people who do not want to speculate with their children's futures. Indeed, a visit to the SavingForCollege Web site showed that many plans suffered in the stock market slide of 2000.

If your own state's plan does not suit you, look at the offerings of another state, even though you may forgo state tax advantages—you need not be a resident of a state to take advantage of the 529 plan it sponsors.

Limitations of the Programs

The account in a Section 529 program can be used only for qualified higher education expenses. If the child for whom the account is set up does not go to college, the account can be transferred to another family member. If there is no other child in the family whom the donor wishes to benefit, then the owner must generally pay income tax and a penalty, usually 10 percent, to liquidate the account. (In case of an emergency, this can be an advantage, rather than a limitation, because the owner could at least get to the money, again paying the tax and penalty on any withdrawal.) Some states, including Colorado, New York, Tennessee, Washington, and Wisconsin, impose a waiting period of two years or more before money can be distributed from the accounts.

Transferring Long-Term Capital Gains to the Child

BOTH SERIES I BONDS AND SECTION 529 programs have been in existence only a few years. Many parents of teenagers have saved for their children's educations by accumulating assets in regular, taxable accounts, and here is a strategy to keep as much as possible after taxes. As a result of the Taxpayer Relief Act of 1997, an 8 percent rate on capital gains realized on assets held five years or more came into effect in 2001 for taxpayers in the 15 percent bracket on ordinary income. A corresponding cut to 18 percent on capital gains on assets held five years or more for those in tax brackets above that level takes effect in 2006.

If an executive in the 38.6 percent bracket, for example, has been accumulating shares over the years, she can transfer some of the shares with a low basis to her daughter, who is entering college. The child will get her mother's cost basis and the benefit of her mother's long-term holding period, and if the child has little or no other income, she can sell the shares to help pay college costs and will owe only the 8 percent tax on the gains, whereas her mother would have had to pay 20 percent. Annual gifts of up to $10,000 would have no gift-tax consequence, and a couple could give up to $20,000 per recipient.

What's more, although the executive's adjusted gross income exceeds the income limit to claim the Hope tax credit for her daughter, she can, via election, waive the dependency exemption for her daughter. In her bracket, she would lose part of the value of the exemption anyway. Then the child can also claim a $1,500 Hope credit on her own return, Mr. Kess, a New York tax attorney and CPA, points out. Credits reduce taxes dollar for dollar.

Funding Education IRAs

EDUCATION IRAS, DESPITE THE TAX-FREE withdrawals they offer—like a Roth, after-tax money goes in, and distributions for qualified educational expenses are tax-free—had found little favor among tax professionals since they were authorized by the 1997 tax law, but the 2001 tax act has made them considerably more attractive. Although there are still some strings attached, the contribution limit has been raised to $2,000 from the previous $500 a year, and corporations will be able to contribute to education IRAs for the benefit of their employees. Also, the income limits for contributors are being raised. (Beginning in 2002 joint filers with modified AGI of $190,000, phasing out at $220,000, are able to contribute, compared with the previous $150,000, phasing out at $160,000.)

Furthermore, contributions may now be made to an education IRA and to a Section 529 program in the same year for the same beneficiary (previously they could not be). And the act expands the definition of qualified education expenses to include elementary and secondary school expenses. Finally, beginning in 2002 individuals can exclude education IRA distributions from gross income and claim Hope or lifetime learning credits in the same year, provided they are not used for the same educational expenses.

Withdrawing Money from Regular IRAs

PARENTS MAY ALSO WITHDRAW MONEY from traditional and Roth IRAs to pay qualifying education expenses for their children without incurring the additional 10 percent tax penalty that is normally levied on withdrawals by people under age 59½.

Borrowing from Retirement Plans

ANOTHER TAX-ADVANTAGED STRATEGY is to borrow from a qualified retirement plan or 401(k) tax-deferred retirement plan. There are three reasons to borrow, rather than make early withdrawals, from the plan. First, because there are annual contribution limits to the plans, a person who is already making the maximum contribution cannot make up for a withdrawal by contributing more in future years. Repaying a loan, however, does not count against these limits. Furthermore, the interest you pay on the loan is paid to your account, not to an outside lender, such as a bank.

Second, a withdrawal is taxable when made, and if the account holder is under age 59½, it is subject to a 10 percent penalty as well. A loan, however, has no such tax consequence or penalty.

The third reason applies to middle-income families whose children may qualify for colleges' financial aid packages. When investments are legally owned by children, as they are in most tax-advantaged education plans, these holdings may work against them when the aid package is calculated. The value of parents' retirement plans, however, will not count against the children. Moreover, the annual contribution to the plan will keep down the family's adjusted gross income, increasing the child's chances for a favorable aid package.

Highlights of Tax Benefits for Higher Education

The I.R.S. cautions, "You generally cannot claim more than one benefit for the same education expense." Details of the benefits are explained in Publication 970.

	Hope Credit	Lifetime Learning Credit	Education IRA
What is your benefit?	Credits can reduce the amount of tax you must pay	Credits can reduce the amount of tax you must pay	Earnings are not taxed
What is the annual limit?	Up to $1,500 per student	Up to $1,000 per family	$2,000 contribution per beneficiar
What expenses qualify besides tuition and required enrollment fees?	None	None	Books, supplie and equipmen Room and boar at least a hal time student. Payments to sta tuition progran
What education qualifies?	First 2 years of undergraduate	All undergraduate and graduate	All undergradua and graduate beginning in 20 elementary an secondary expenses as we
What are some of the other conditions that apply?	Can be claimed for only 2 years. Must be enrolled at least half-time in a degree program.		Beginning in 20 can contribute education IRA a state tuition program in th same year. Must withdrav assets at age 3

1. Any nontaxable withdrawal is limited to the amount that does not exceed qualifying educational expenses.

itional & th IRAs[1]	Student Loan Interest	State Tuition Programs (Section 529)	Education Savings Bond Program[1]	Employer's Educational Assist Program[1]
o 10% tional tax n early hdrawal	You can deduct the interest	Earnings are not taxed	Interest is not taxed	Employer benefits are not taxed
nount of alifying penses	$2,000	None	Amount of qualifying expenses	$5,250
Books, olies, and ipment. and board t least a lf-time tudent.	Books, supplies, and equipment. Room and board. Transportation. Other necessary expenses.	Books, supplies, and equipment. Room and board if at least a half-time student.	Payments to education IRAs. Payments to state tuition programs.	Books, supplies, and equipment.
under-uate and aduate	All undergraduate and graduate	All undergraduate and graduate	All undergraduate and graduate	Undergraduate
	Applies to first 60 months of required interest. Must have been at least half-time student in a degree program.	Beginning in 2002 withdrawn earnings will be tax-free to beneficiary.	Applies only to qualified Series EE bonds issued after 1989 or Series I bonds.	Expires for courses beginning after Dec. 31, 2001.

Internal Revenue Service

(continued on the following page)

125

Highlights of Tax Benefits for Higher Education
(continued)

	Hope Credit	Lifetime Learning Credit	Education IR
In what income range do benefits phase out?	$40,000 to $50,000; $80,000 to $100,000 for joint returns	$40,000 to $50,000; $80,000 to $100,000 for joint returns	$95,000 to $110,000 fc single filers $190,000 t $220,000 fc joint returns beginning in 2002

1. Any nontaxable withdrawal is limited to the amount that does not exceed qualifying educational expenses.

Working with the "Kiddie Tax" Rules

BECAUSE TAX-ADVANTAGED INVESTMENTS for college generally have strings attached and often involve putting the investments in the child's name rather than in the parents', some people have chosen to invest in regular accounts, despite the resultant higher taxes. But it is useful to take the tax laws—specifically the "kiddie tax rules"—into account when planning.

Investment income above $1,500 received by children under age fourteen is taxed at their parents' marginal rate. But the first $750 of income earned on investments in the child's name is tax-free, and the next $750 is taxed at the child's marginal rate—10 percent beginning in 2002 for children who have no other income. This means that the tax owed on interest or dividends of $1,500 and paid to a child would be only $75; if

Traditional & Roth IRAs[1]	Student Loan Interest	State Tuition Programs (Section 529)	Education Savings Bond Program[1]	Employer's Educational Assist Program[1]
There is no phaseout	$50,000 to $65,000 for single taxpayers beginning in 2002; $100,000 to $130,000 for joint returns	There is no phaseout	$54,100 to $69,100; $81,100 to $111,100 for joint returns	There is no phaseout

that same interest and dividends went to a parent in the top bracket of 38.6 percent, the tax liability would be $579. Therefore, it may be worthwhile to put enough in the child's name to take advantage of this break—$25,000 of bonds yielding 6 percent would pay interest of $1,500 a year.

Once people have put enough into the children's names to generate income above $1,500, they often put the rest of their college savings in their own names. Theoretically this money should tilt toward growth stocks that do not pay dividends, which would be taxable as ordinary income. The hope is to realize a big capital gain when it is time for college. Remember, if the stocks are then given to a child aged fourteen or older who has little or no other income, and the child then sells them, the gain, based on current law, would be taxed at only 8 percent.

Investing in Zero-Coupon Municipal Bonds

RISK-AVERSE PARENTS MAY WORRY that stocks are too volatile or uncertain for college savings. An attractive investment for these parents is zero-coupon municipal bonds with maturities timed for each year of college. The parents know precisely how much they will have, and if their children do not attend college or if they win scholarships, they can use the money for other purposes. The disadvantage, of course, is that the bonds pay interest at a much lower rate than the alternatives, and you must make a judgment call as to what college will cost, say, eighteen years in the future.

WHICHEVER PLAN YOU CHOOSE, start saving early. Remember, time is your ally in investing, and the goal you are trying to reach is sizable. According to the College Board, in Princeton, New Jersey, each year since the 1980s college costs have been climbing two or three times as much as the rise in the consumer price index. The College Board calculates that in the 2000–2001 academic year, on average it cost $9,174 at a public four-year college for tuition, room, board, books, and supplies, and $23,271 at a private college. That included costs for tuition and fees of $16,332 at a private four-year college and $3,510 at a public institution. By way of comparison, using constant dollars, the cost of tuition and fees was $7,634 at a private four-year college in 1971–72, the board said, and $1,577 at a four-year public college. Given this trend of escalating costs, it would be a shame not to take advantage of the tax breaks available to save for college.

CHAPTER 9

The Double Life
of Life Insurance

MANY PEOPLE THINK OF life insurance as an important part of their investment portfolios, and if they have cash-value insurance that they purchased before June 21, 1988, they may well be right. Even coverage purchased since then may also do double duty as an investment, although the situation is more complex, as we will explain.

If you are considering buying an insurance policy for its investment value, remember our advice from Chapter 1, "Choosing Your Investment Tools Carefully." Thanks to the tax laws, there are specific situations in which an insurance product may be an appropriate investment tool. But because of the expenses involved, insurance products are not generally likely to provide an after-tax return that is competitive with that of a pure investment product. (The primary reason to buy life insurance, after all, is to provide protection for dependents or a business should you die, but choosing the right insurance product can be complicated and is beyond the scope of this book. We are looking only at how the tax laws treat the investment aspects of insurance.)

Permanent Life's Impermanent Benefits

BROADLY SPEAKING, THERE ARE two basic types of life insurance: term and permanent. Term insurance—so named because it is in effect for a set time period—costs less and provides only a death benefit. It is often the choice of young parents, for example, who want to be sure money will be available for their children if one or both of the parents die before their children are self-sufficient. Once the children are grown and no longer need that safety net, the parents can discontinue the coverage.

Permanent life insurance, which includes whole life, universal life, and variable life, not only provides a death benefit but also has a cash value that accumulates in an investment account. Permanent life insurance is more expensive than term life, but premiums are fixed, rather than rising as the policyholder gets older. After time the earnings from the investment account will generally more than cover the premium, ending that annual cash outlay and allowing the cash value to grow. Significantly, that inside buildup is tax-free, as are death benefits. Thus, permanent life insurance could be ideal for a business owner, for example, who wants to be able to leave her business intact to her children. They could use the tax-free proceeds of the insurance policy to pay estate taxes on the business, so that they would not have to sell parts of the business. Estate taxes are to be with us through the year 2009, disappear in 2010, and unless a new tax law is passed, reappear in 2011 (see Appendix 2). That, of course, makes estate planning a bit of a sticky wicket.

The Lure: Tax Benefits

For many people the great lure of permanent life insurance traditionally was not its death benefit but ancillary benefits that they themselves could enjoy: Policyholders can withdraw money up to the amount of the premiums they have paid or borrow against the cash value of the policy, generally at very low rates in comparison with other loans. Furthermore, for pre-1988 policies, the loan is not treated as taxable income. Should the policyholder die before repaying the loan, the insurer simply deducts any outstanding debt from the death benefit.

In the 1980s, life insurance companies and brokerage houses began to exploit the tax benefits that life insurance offered. They focused a selling effort on single-premium life insurance contracts that often promised 8 or 9 percent annual returns. Most of the premium went into the policy's cash value, not into its insurance component.

Say a fifty-year-old man bought a single-premium policy for $100,000. He could look forward to seeing the cash value grow to $200,000 before he was sixty years old and $400,000 well before he was seventy. He could tap into it by withdrawing money and taking tax-free loans of perhaps $30,000 a year for life and still leave enough in the policy to provide a tax-free insurance payout for his beneficiaries.

It seemed too good to be true, and indeed, the IRS complained to Congress, which rewrote the law, imposing what was known as the "seven-pay test." Policies sold after June 21, 1988, must pass that test to qualify for tax-free loans and withdrawals. The law requires that premiums be paid over a series of years, typically at least seven (hence the name), if the policy is to be classified as insurance and get the tax benefits of insurance.

Modified Endowment Contracts

Policies, such as single-premium contracts, that fail the test are classified not as insurance but as modified endowment contracts, often known as MECs. Say someone puts $100,000 into a MEC, and several years later the value has grown to $200,000. He then wants to withdraw $125,000. Under the law, the accumulated earnings come out first, so $100,000 is treated as taxable earnings, and $25,000 is treated as a withdrawal of money he put in. The tax treatment is similar to that for an IRA or qualified retirement plan in that the earnings are taxable at current rates, and if the person is under age 59½, he is subject to a 10 percent tax penalty as well. If a policyholder assigns or pledges the policy as collateral for a loan, it is treated as a distribution for tax purposes.

Although the "seven-pay" test was a setback, Congress certainly did not close the door completely to tax-advantaged insurance investment products, and the industry still offers them, the best known being tax-deferred annuities.

Tax-Deferred Annuities

TAX-DEFERRED ANNUITIES, which are underwritten by insurance companies, come in two forms, fixed and variable, and are essentially supplemental retirement plans. Fixed annuities are so named because they provide fixed income. Variable annuities are generally clones of popular mutual funds with an insurance wrapper. Investors may either pay a one-time lump sum to purchase an annuity or they may make installment payments. The interest, dividends, and capital gains accumulate on a tax-deferred basis until they are paid out to the investor. Again, if a person under age 59½ withdraws money, it is subject to both income taxes and a 10 percent penalty.

The Pros and Cons

The selling point for annuities obviously is tax deferral. They can be particularly attractive to someone who has not taken advantage of qualified retirement plans until relatively late in life and therefore needs to put away more than is possible through whatever tax-deferred plans are available.

For example, say a fifty-year-old woman who changed jobs several times before becoming vested in a company pension plan and previously gave little thought to the matter has now decided she wants to retire at age sixty. She earns a good income and is now contributing as much as is allowed both to her 401(k) plan and to a Keogh plan for some sideline consulting income. But ten years of contributions to these plans will not provide enough to fund what could well be a thirty-year retirement. She must put away more, so a tax-deferred annuity is an attractive option.

But the price can be high, so annuities should be considered only as a long-term investment. There may be sales commissions for the contracts themselves, as well as management and administrative fees and the cost of life insurance for the death benefits the contracts promise—all in addition to the fees charged by the funds within the contract. And if an investor wants to get out of a contract early, there may be an additional charge for that. "Because of these higher costs, variable annuities are generally worthwhile only if you have fully utilized all other available tax-deferred retirement vehicles, such as IRAs and 401(k)s," the Vanguard Group of Investing Companies advises.[1] "At the minimum, you should expect to keep your annuity investment for twenty years, since it can easily take that long before the benefits of tax deferral outweigh the added costs of the annuity."

The accounting firm Price Waterhouse (now Pricewater-houseCoopers) calculated that the break-even point for a variable annuity for a person in the 39.6 percent tax bracket would be twenty years if the annuity earned 10 percent a year, and thirty-nine years if it earned 7 percent, assuming an annuity expense of 1 percent.[2] For a person in the 28 percent bracket, the break-even points are twelve years at 10 percent and twenty-nine years at 7 percent. Although tax rates for 2002 are down 1 percentage point from those rates, that is not a big enough change to make a significant difference in the results of the study.

Therefore, for investors who are eligible for Roth IRAs, establishing a Roth should come ahead of purchasing an annuity. And even for those who are not eligible for Roths, annuities may not be the most attractive supplemental retirement savings plan.

Martin Nissenbaum, national director of retirement planning for Ernst & Young, said he occasionally recommends annuities but added, "You can basically create your own annuity" by investing in a fund that mimics the Standard & Poor's 500 stock index.[3] There is very little current capital gains tax with such a holding, he noted, because the portfolio turnover is minimal, and when you sell holdings after retirement, any capital gains are taxed at favorable rates. In contrast, any money that comes out of qualified plans or IRAs is taxed as ordinary income, as is the money from variable annuities.

MECs Revisited

If investors need money during their lifetime, withdrawals from either a deferred annuity or a modified endowment contract will be subject both to income tax and to a 10 percent penalty if they are under age 59½, but many people do not make lifetime withdrawals, preferring to leave the money untapped, if they can afford to do so, so that it can go to their heirs. In that case, a MEC is preferable to an annuity. The annuity is merely tax-deferred, not tax-free. In contrast, under the tax laws a MEC is treated like insurance. Not only is no income tax due on the buildup, but also beneficiaries must receive a death benefit that is greater than the cash value, and that death benefit will be tax-free to them.

Variable Life Insurance

IF YOUR MAIN GOAL IS to leave money to heirs, variable life insurance is preferable to either tax-deferred annuities or MECs. As with variable annuities, the cash value of variable life policies may be invested in mutual funds, and the policyholder directs the investments, or it may be placed with investment managers. Any growth depends on how well the funds do. But even if they do poorly, the insurance company guarantees a minimum death benefit.

Like other forms of permanent life insurance, variable life offers tax-free buildup of cash value, tax-free loans and withdrawals, and death benefits that are free of income tax. That is in stark contrast to an annuity—income and estate taxes could take nearly 70 percent of an annuity's value before beneficiaries receive anything, unless of course the death occurs in 2010.

If you want to maintain control over the variable life policy and therefore retain ownership of it, the policy will be included in your estate, which will make it subject to estate taxes if you die before 2010, and possibly if you die after that unless the repeal of the death tax is extended.

135

Because the 2001 law is to be phased in over several years, an older person, especially one in failing health, might consider it prudent to plan for the eventuality of estate taxes while getting his affairs in order.

That said, we will discuss a strategy for avoiding both estate and income taxes on benefits paid by variable life insurance policies.

Putting a Variable Life Policy in an Irrevocable Life Insurance Trust

By investing through a variable life insurance policy inside an irrevocable life insurance trust, you can potentially eliminate both the income tax on investment earnings and estate taxes on the funds distributed to beneficiaries. If your main objective is to leave money to the next generation, you can choose to maintain your variable life investments within the irrevocable trust until death. You would also be able to retain access to professional investment managers. With a domestic variable life insurance policy, you can select from a suite of mutual funds. With an offshore variable life insurance policy, the policy's investment managers may also include hedge-fund and other alternative-investment managers, as well as your current investment manager or managers.

If a variable life insurance policy is purchased by a third party, such as an irrevocable life insurance trust, the death benefit, then, should escape both estate tax on the death of the insured and the generation-skipping transfer tax on the death of the insured's children (up to the applicable generation-skipping tax limit). Because the federal rates of each of these taxes for 2002 can reach up to 50 percent, the potential tax savings are substantial.

Establishing a variable life insurance policy within a trust typically involves the following six steps:

1 Husband and wife set up an irrevocable life insurance trust for the benefit of their children and hire a professional trustee.

2 Husband and wife donate cash to the trust.

3 The trust uses the cash to purchase a variable life insurance policy from a licensed insurance company.

4 The investment portion of the premium is placed in a custodial account.

5 The investment portion of the premium is invested with one or more investment managers who are approved by the insurance company and selected by the trustee (that is, the policyholder).

6 On the death of the insured, the assets in the variable life insurance policy pass to the irrevocable life insurance trust free of income and estate taxes.

If there is not already a trust with sufficient assets to purchase the policy, the insured will need to make one or more gifts to the trust to enable it to purchase the variable life insurance policy. The gift(s) could be significant in some cases and could require the payment of a gift tax. Even so, the gift tax paid currently (prior to the inside buildup) could be much less than the estate tax that would otherwise be due at the insured's death (after the inside buildup), if the death occurs before 2010 or if the estate tax is resumed after that year.

Investors who have concentrated stock holdings with a low cost basis and who wish to diversify through a variable life insurance policy will first have to raise cash to purchase a policy, either by selling their holdings and reinvesting the after-tax proceeds or by utilizing one or more of the strategies that enable investors to hedge and monetize appreciated securities without becoming liable for a current tax (as discussed in Chapters 5 and 11). Note, however, that some people believe it is possible to accomplish a non-taxed transfer by using a "private annuity" structure—that is, transfers from a stock portfolio into an annuity that is owned by an irrevocable life insurance trust.

Choosing between Domestic and Offshore Policies

Insurance can provide an investor with additional asset protection. For maximum protection, the insurance company should be chartered and licensed in a country (such as the United States or a number of foreign jurisdictions) that provides for the establishment of "segregated accounts." These "segregated account rules" provide that not only are funds in the segregated account of the insurance company generally not exposed to creditors' claims against the insurer but also that these funds are generally protected from the claims of creditors of the insured and of the policyholder (that is, the trust). In an offshore variable life insurance policy the assets are typically held by a blue-chip custodian and secured so that neither the insurance company nor any third party, without the permission of the policyholder, may remove the assets.

When comparing and contrasting domestic and offshore policies, you should consider investment flexibility, regulatory constraints, front-end costs, and asset protection. Offshore policies offer investors a greater degree of flexibility than domestic policies, both in regard to what investments are permitted and to the selection of investment managers; domestic policies must comply with stringent state insurance laws. As noted previously, in an offshore policy, the manager can include hedge-fund and other alternative-investment managers, as well as the investor's current investment manager or managers.

You should, however, balance the increased investment flexibility of an offshore variable life insurance policy against the looser regulatory framework of a less stringently regulated foreign jurisdiction. Also, consider how much confidence you have in a particular foreign country's legal system or political stability before investing in a policy that originates there. You may be able to mitigate legal and political risk by using a blue-chip custodian.

Offshore variable life insurance policies can be significantly less expensive than domestic policies because of lower excise taxes, wholesale-level commission rates, and lower regulatory expenses. As stated previously they also offer the possibility of additional protection against creditor claims.

Non-Tax Disadvantages of Variable Life

Before investing, you should consider the several nontax disadvantages associated with variable life insurance policies. You have less control over your assets inside a variable life insurance policy than outside. Further, the policies are potentially subject to a series of revenue rulings the IRS issued in the late 1970s and early 1980s known as the "investor control" rulings. Under these rulings, if the policyholder has sufficient control to direct investments made in the insurance company's separate account, the policyholder, rather than the insurance company, could be treated for tax purposes as the owner of the assets held in the segregated account. The policyholder would therefore be taxed currently on the inside buildup.

The point at which a variable life insurance policy runs afoul of the investor control rulings is not clear. Although the degree of investor control varies from insurer to insurer and policy to policy, it is better to opt for too little investor control than too much, given the potentially severe tax consequences of too much control. And if that seems troublesome, remember that any other way in which you might plan for a tax-efficient transfer of assets from one generation to the next (to remove the assets from the investor's estate), you would also be quite likely to have to minimize your control of the assets.

Finally, although the up-front costs and annual expense charges make investing through a variable life insurance policy considerably more expensive than investing outside the policy, the potential tax benefits typically outweigh these increased costs.

IN CERTAIN SITUATIONS—putting together supplemental retirement funds while providing for heirs or arranging to bequeath a family business unfettered by estate taxes—insurance products are the best tool. Still, remember the adage that insurance is sold, not bought. Before saying yes to a sales pitch, be sure that the tax and other benefits of the particular insurance product you are considering will outweigh the additional costs of the product, as compared with a simpler, more conventional investment.

PART 3

Special
Situations

CHAPTER 10

Making

Prudent Elections

T HE NATION'S TAX LAWS are not nearly so rigid as taxpayers often assume. Among the tax code's provisions are numerous "elections" that allow taxpayers to choose one tax treatment over another. A wise choice can often lower or defer your tax liability.

The elections described below highlight a few of the important tax-saving choices you can make. Remember that the very reason for elections is that what works best for one taxpayer may not work best for another, and compared with some tax elections, a Florida ballot is child's play, so before making an election, discuss your particular facts and circumstances with your tax adviser.

Writing a Letter to Your Broker

WHEN SELLING PART OF A HOLDING, investors are allowed to elect which shares to sell. Because investors generally want to keep taxable capital gains as low as possible, a simple way to make this election is to write a letter to your broker giving a standing instruction that when part of a holding is sold, the highest-cost-basis long-term shares are to be delivered unless a specific written instruction to the contrary is made at the time of the sale.

In the absence of a written instruction to sell particular shares, the IRS assumes you delivered the shares that were acquired first.

Say an investor first purchased 1,000 shares of XYZ ten years ago, when it was trading at $10. The stock price has steadily risen by $10 a year, and every year she has added 1,000 shares to her position, so that in the year 2000, she paid $100,000 for 1,000 shares, or $100 per share. Now she wants to sell 1,000 shares. Assuming that (1) she has written the letter, (2) she has held the shares she acquired in 2000 more than a year, and (3) XYZ is now trading at $110, her capital gain will be $10,000, on which she will owe taxes of $2,000. If she has failed to write the blanket-instruction letter or a specific letter pertaining to this sale, her broker will sell the first shares she purchased, resulting in a capital gain of $100,000 and a tax bill of $20,000.

Of course, there may be times when an investor will want to countermand the general letter. Say the XYZ shareholder had a real dog in her portfolio. She might sell it and take the opportunity to sell her low-basis XYZ shares, using her loss on DOG to offset the gain on XYZ. But more often investors prefer to limit taxable capital gains, so the standing instruction is advisable.

Amortizing Bond Premiums

WHEN A BOND IS PURCHASED in the secondary market at more than its face or par value, the difference between the two amounts is a bond premium. Section 171 of the Internal

Revenue Code allows bondholders to elect to amortize the premium—that is, deduct a ratable portion of it annually until the bond matures.

Amortizing the premium will give you annual deductions against ordinary income and reduce your basis in the bond so that at maturity you will have neither a gain nor a loss on the bond. If you do not elect to amortize the premium, your purchase price will continue to be your basis in the bond, so that when it matures, the difference will constitute a capital loss, which often is not as advantageous as a deduction against ordinary income.

This election is available only for taxable bonds, not for tax-exempts. If it is made, it affects all similar bonds in a portfolio. To make the election, simply take the deduction on your tax return.

Making Elections Regarding Bond Discounts

A BOND OR NOTE MAY BE DISCOUNTED to its par value either because it was issued at a discount to face value—as are Treasury bills, zero-coupon corporate bonds, and Series EE (and their predecessor Series E) U.S. savings bonds—or because it has declined in price in the market. Treasury bonds, for example, are issued with a par value of $100, but when interest rates rise, bond prices decline, so when rates are on the upswing, bonds trading in the secondary market are priced at a discount.

Generally, holders of original-issue discount (OID) bonds, other than savings bonds, must report part of the OID as interest income each year they hold the bond, even though they will not actually receive the money until the bond is cashed in at maturity.

For market-discount issues, however, the discount is normally reported when you sell the bond, but you may elect to treat all interest on a debt instrument acquired during the tax year as OID and include it in income annually. The election will apply to all market-discount bonds you may subsequently acquire, and you may not revoke it without IRS consent. The election could be beneficial if you want to accelerate income for any of the reasons discussed elsewhere in this book.

Holders of savings bonds may also elect to report their imputed interest annually rather than recognizing it all when the bonds mature. This could be advantageous for investors who expect to be in a substantially higher tax bracket when the bond matures.

Another election affects how to report market discount. Typically, the straight-line or ratable accrual method is used, but bondholders may elect to use the compound or constant-yield method, which is generally preferable because it results in a smaller accrual of taxable market discount. If this election is made, it may not be changed.

Making the Mixed-Straddle Election

A STRADDLE IS A POSITION that offsets another position an investor holds in personal property other than stock. A straddle is mixed when the two positions are subject to different rules. For example, say an investor bought a SPDR, which is an exchange fund that mimics the S&P 500 stock index and is not subject to marked-to-market rules, and hedged the purchase by selling options on the S&P 500 index. These options are Section 1256 assets (as are regulated futures contracts and foreign currency contracts), and as such are subject to the marked-to-market rules. This means that gains or losses on options must be reported annually and are arbitrarily considered 40 percent short term and 60 percent long term.

If the SPDR declines, then, as is the case for any stock, no loss will be recognized until it is sold, which need not be in the current year. But as the underlying instrument drops, the options' position gains value, so the investor could be left with a current-year gain from marking to market the options and no current-year loss against which to take it.

Making the mixed-straddle election on Form 6781 provides a way around this sticky wicket. By making the election, the investor could recognize the gain and the loss simultaneously.

Claiming a Foreign Tax Credit

MANY FOREIGN COUNTRIES WITHHOLD taxes on dividend and interest payments. At a time when many investors consider global investing to be an important part of portfolio diversification, that means many American investors have paid foreign taxes. If you are one of them, you must still report the dividend or interest to the IRS, but the foreign tax may reduce your American taxes in one of two ways.

You can elect to report the tax as an itemized deduction on Schedule A, or you can claim a foreign tax credit on Form 1116. Generally a credit is better because it offsets taxes dollar for dollar, whereas the value of a deduction is determined by your marginal rate. Thus, for a top-bracket taxpayer, a $100 credit is more than two and a half times as valuable as a $100 deduction. However, because of the limitations on Form 1116, some taxpayers may find they cannot take the credit; in that case, the deduction is better than nothing at all.

Avoiding Claiming a Child's Unearned Income

FOR THE YEAR 2001, unearned income (such as interest and dividends) of children under age fourteen in excess of $1,500 is taxable at their parents' marginal rate. If a child has such investment income, a tax return must be filed for the child. Alternatively, the parents may elect to claim the child's unearned income on their own return. To make this election, they must attach Form 8814 to their return.

The election will save the paperwork of filling out returns for children. Upper-income taxpayers, however, should be aware that making this election will also raise their own adjusted gross income (AGI), and that can have adverse consequences. For example, including your child's interest and dividends in your AGI may raise it to the point where personal exemptions and itemized deductions are phased out. Certain itemized deductions may be taken only to the extent they exceed specified floors: 7.5 percent of AGI for medical deductions and 2 percent of AGI for miscellaneous itemized deductions.

Electing to Defer Capital Gains

AN INDIVIDUAL OR A C corporation can elect to defer recognition of a capital gain, subject to certain limitations, that is realized on the sale of publicly traded securities if the proceeds of the sale are used within sixty days to purchase common stock or a partnership interest in a specialized small business investment company. You postpone the gain by adjusting the basis of the replacement property. In effect, you defer your gain until the year you dispose of the replacement property.

A specialized small business investment company (SSBIC) is any partnership or corporation licensed under Section 301(d) of the Small Business Investment Act of 1958 as in effect on May 13, 1993. For most individuals, the lesser of $50,000 or $500,000 reduced by any previously deferred gain can be rolled over in one tax year. For C corporations, the numbers are $250,000 or $1 million.

To make the election, you should report the entire gain realized from the sale of the publicly traded securities on Schedule D of Form 1040 and write "SSBIC Rollover" directly below the line on which you reported the gain. You should enter the amount of the postponed gain as a loss, thereby canceling out the gain reported on the line above. You should also attach a schedule showing the following: how you figured the postponed gain, the name of the SSBIC in which you purchased common stock or a partnership interest, the date of that purchase, and your new basis in that SSBIC stock or partnership interest.

You must make the choice to postpone the gain by the due date (including extensions) of the tax return on which you must report the gain. Your choice is revocable with the consent of the IRS.

Caution on Electing to Be a Trader

PEOPLE WHO ACTIVELY BUY AND SELL stocks, especially to take advantage of short-term market swings, would appear to have an attractive election under Section 475 of the Internal Revenue Code: the election to be a trader rather than an investor.

One difference from a tax standpoint is that an investor is allowed to claim a miscellaneous itemized deduction for such expenses as accounting, legal, investment-management, or investment-planning fees; subscriptions to investment services; secretarial or bookkeeping help; and depreciation on a computer used to manage investments. But miscellaneous itemized deductions may be taken only to the extent that they total more than 2 percent of adjusted gross income.

For example, an investor who had an AGI of $200,000 could take a miscellaneous itemized deduction only to the extent it exceeded $4,000. If he had $2,000 worth of investment expenses and $1,500 worth of other miscellaneous itemized deductions, such as dues to a professional organization, he could not take a miscellaneous itemized deduction. If his AGI were $100,000 and he had the same expenses, he could deduct $1,500—the amount by which his expenses exceeded a 2 percent threshold of $2,000.

A trader, however, is not subject to these limitations. A trader is considered to be in the trade or business of trading and therefore can deduct all of his expenses against his profit, which he would report by filing Schedule C of Form 1040 as a self-employed person. As a self-employed person he may also be entitled to claim a home-office deduction, which is not allowed investors.

But many people who elect to be traders find the IRS disallows their elections, and courts have backed the Service. "Note that recent court cases require that, to qualify as a trader, you must do transactions for others, not just yourself," the accounting firm Deloitte & Touche has advised its clients.

Making the Deemed-Sale Election

UNDER A PROVISION OF THE Taxpayer Relief Act of 1997 that became effective for assets acquired in 2001 and later, taxpayers in the regular tax brackets of 28 percent and higher will have a second long-term capital gains rate: 18 percent for assets held five years or longer. These taxpayers will not actually benefit from the pared rate until 2006. But if a taxpayer were to sell an asset in 2006 that she had acquired, say, ten years earlier, she would still owe capital gains at the regular long-term capital gains rate of 20 percent, even though she had held it twice as long as another asset acquired in 2001 that qualified for the 18 percent rate. So Congressional tax writers provided a way out of this seemingly unfair situation: the deemed sale.

Under the deemed sale, the investor can elect on her 2001 tax return—to be filed in 2002—to make a deemed sale, valuing the asset as of January 2, 2001, the first day the law took effect. She would pay taxes based on that price, then "buy" the asset back at the same price. Assuming she sold the asset at a profit in 2006, she would then pay taxes at the 18 percent rate on the difference between the 2001 price and her sale price. This is referred to as a deemed sale because the asset is not actually sold and bought back; it is just treated as though it had been on the tax return.

In deciding whether to make this election, investors face the question: Is the tax savings of 2 percentage points (10 percent of the tax) sufficient incentive to pay a capital gains tax five years earlier than I would otherwise have to pay it? If an investor is sitting on a large gain, the answer will generally be no, it is not worth paying the tax in 2002 (unless, of course, he also has a big capital loss he would like to offset). But investors who are about even on a holding or have a small long-term gain (meaning little tax will be due) and are convinced that the longer-term prospects are good may benefit by making the deemed-sale election. If their outlook for the stock proves to be right, taxes owed on gains incurred in and after 2006 will be 10 percent lower than they would otherwise have been.

A calculator that will help stockholders make this decision is available at www.twenty-first.com/calculator.htm. It shows, for example, that if an investor had a stock that closed on January 2, 2001, at $40 and she had a long-term capital gain of $1 in it, she would be glad to have made the deemed sale if the stock climbed to $44.40 or higher by 2006. If her cost basis were $35, the stock would have to climb to $62.02 or higher to make the election a wise choice. If the basis were $20, a climb to $128.07 would be needed.

Among the factors that a taxpayer should consider in deciding whether to make a deemed sale are:

❑ the cost basis of the stock
❑ its current market price
❑ the projected sale price
❑ whether the holding period as of January 1, 2001, is over or under twelve months and thus whether the investor would owe taxes on a short- or long-term capital gain if a deemed sale were made
❑ the projected holding period
❑ state and local taxes
❑ opportunity costs (the profits that the investor could have earned on the taxes paid)

The figure at right shows the break-even points for making the deemed-sale election.

Investors sitting on a large loss should not make a deemed sale, because the loss is neither recognized nor preserved through a basis adjustment. However, if the stock eventually gains value, overcoming the loss position, a stockholder might want to actually sell it and then repurchase it, thereby creating a new holding period eligible for the 18 percent rate. If an

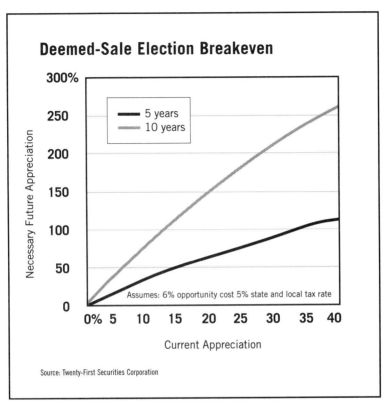

Deemed-Sale Election Breakeven

Source: Twenty-First Securities Corporation

investor has a minimal loss in a position, it may be worthwhile to make the deemed-sale election, because the absence of transaction costs could outweigh forgoing the capital-loss deduction.

Handling Restricted Stock

EXECUTIVES OR EMPLOYEES WHO RECEIVE restricted stock that they expect to appreciate may save on taxes by making a Section 83(b) election. The election converts future appreciation that would otherwise be taxable as ordinary income to capital gains.

Under Section 83 of the Internal Revenue Code, property,

such as restricted stock (but not options), that is received as compensation for services is taxable as ordinary income as soon as it is vested and transferable. But if the property is not transferable and is subject to substantial risk of forfeiture, the owner is not required to recognize the income until at least one of the conditions has lapsed. However, the owner can choose to be taxed immediately by making an 83(b) election within thirty days of receipt of the stock. When an option is exercised, the date of exercise is considered the date the stock is received. The goal is to exercise the option when the spread between the exercise price and the market price is as low as possible to limit the amount that is taxable as ordinary income.

For example, say an executive holds an option entitling him to acquire 5,000 shares at $4 a share. He exercises the option when the stock is trading at $5 a share, so he has spent $20,000 to exercise the option and has restricted stock worth $25,000. He makes an 83(b) election and pays taxes on the $5,000 difference as ordinary income. Say that in two years one of the restrictions on the stock lapses, and it is trading at $20 a share. His holding is worth $100,000, meaning he has a paper gain of $75,000.

Had he delayed recognizing the income for tax purposes until he was legally required to do so, he would now owe taxes on $80,000 worth of ordinary income. Instead, he paid taxes on only $5,000 of ordinary income and can recognize the rest of the appreciation as a long-term gain when he chooses to do so.

Taxpayers will want to exercise options early and make this election—volunteering to pay taxes before they are legally required to do so—only when the tax involved will be small and the prospects for future appreciation are very strong. That is an important caveat because if a taxpayer misjudges a stock's prospects and the price tumbles, no tax loss can be taken on the income that was recognized.

Other Elections Relevant to Tax and Financial Planning

THE ELECTIONS DISCUSSED in this chapter are not the only elections taxpayers may make. Some elections are not related to investments (which sibling of several who signed a multiple-support agreement for an elderly parent will take a dependency exemption, for example). Other elections, because they affect a person's overall asset allocation, are relevant in terms of tax and financial planning. Depending on personal circumstances they may be worth discussing with your tax adviser, even though they are not directly related to investment portfolios. Among them are the following:

❑ **Electing out of an installment sale.** If you sell an asset (a plant or business equipment, for example) and agree to accept payment for it in installments, you must use the installment method to report the income received unless you elect on your tax return, pursuant to Section 453(d)(2), not to use that method. If you make the election, you generally report the entire gain in the year of sale, even though you will not be paid the selling price in that year. This election does not apply to marketable securities.

❑ **Electing to aggregate rental properties.** Real estate professionals may make an election under Section 469(c)(7)(A) to aggregate their rental properties, treating all interests in real estate as a single activity. That way the individual rental properties will not be treated as passive, and the owners will be able to take the losses against other income.

❑ **Elections regarding lump-sum pension distributions.** If you receive a lump-sum distribution from a qualified

155

retirement plan (but not an IRA) and the plan participant
was born before 1936, you may elect to have any of the
money that resulted from active participation in the plan
before 1974 treated as a capital gain subject to a 20 percent tax rate; the rest would be taxed as ordinary income.
You may also elect to use the ten-year tax option to figure
tax on the part that is ordinary income. You pay the tax
only for the year in which you receive the distribution, but
it is calculated as though it were received over ten years.
Both optional methods are reported on Form 4972.

IF YOU CAST YOUR BALLOT WISELY in the elections described in
this chapter, you will have more of your money available to live
on or to invest, and the IRS will get less of it.

CHAPTER 11

Managing

Your Employee

Stock Options

STOCK OPTIONS, WHICH HAVE BECOME an increasingly significant part of executive compensation packages in recent years, are governed by complex and arcane tax rules that require careful study if an executive wants to lock in value in a volatile market.

The widespread confusion that exists about options and the rules governing them was evident after President George W. Bush chose Dick Cheney, then chairman of Halliburton, as his running mate. If Mr. Cheney, as vice president, continued to hold his Halliburton options, it would constitute a conflict of interest. If he simply walked away from them, he would be leaving a substantial amount of money on the table. So his problem was how, under the tax laws, to extract value by hedging the holding while avoiding any conflict of interest.

The news reports that discussed the matter and possible strategies contained as much misinformation as information. Mr. Cheney, who said he would be willing to walk away from the options, did not announce whether he had done so or had found another solution.

Hedging Option Holdings to Lock In Value

ALTHOUGH MOST EXECUTIVES will not face the particular conflict-of-interest issues that Vice President Cheney faced, many do face the issue of how to hedge their option holdings to lock in value. Their hope, of course, is that the underlying stock will climb in value, enabling the option holder to buy shares at a substantial discount to the market price. But if the stock price slides, the option's value slides, too. The problem is how to hedge the option position to lock in value.

Before an option holder is vested, there is really nothing concrete to hedge; trying to construct a hedge then amounts to a speculation. But once an option holder is vested, it is possible to construct a hedge that protects the value of the holdings without incurring any tax liability. However, choosing the right hedge can be complicated.

Tax Consequences

THE TAX CONSEQUENCES OF HEDGING employee stock options could very well mirror those of hedging the underlying stock. Section 1259 of the Internal Revenue Code sets out conditions in which a taxpayer will be treated as having constructively sold an "appreciated financial position"—that is, a position in which there would be a gain should it be sold, assigned, or otherwise terminated at its fair market value. In the absence of IRS rulings or court decisions to settle the matter, some practitioners contend that employee stock options are not subject to the constructive-sale rules. (See Chapter 5 for a detailed discussion of these rules.) We take the more conservative position that employee stock options *are* covered by the constructive-sale rules.

Those who contend that employee stock options are not subject to the constructive-sale rules point out that if the option is terminated at its fair market value, the termination will give rise to compensation income, as opposed to "gain." Throughout the tax code, the word "gain" is used when an asset is disposed of, typically in a capital transaction. This distinction between gain and compensation is the basis for the conclusion held by some that employee stock options are not governed by the constructive-sale rules.

However, Section 1001 defines "gain" as the excess of the amount realized over the basis in the asset that is disposed of. The IRS defines basis as "the amount of your investment in property for tax purposes," adding, "The basis of property you buy is usually the cost. Basis is used to figure gain or loss on the sale or disposition of investment property." Thus, while there would be gain on the disposition of an option, inasmuch as the holder has received it from an employer rather than purchasing it, that gain would probably be treated as compensation income. That is why we will assume that all employee stock options are covered by the constructive-sale rules.

Basic Option Hedges

ASSUMING THAT EMPLOYEE STOCK OPTIONS are covered by the constructive-sale rules, the hedging transaction must be carefully structured so that it does not result in a taxable gain by making sure it does not eliminate nearly all the risk of loss or potential for gain in the stock options.

In general, the two basic hedging strategies, as detailed in Chapter 5, are short sales and collars. Short sales are not appropriate hedges for employee stock options, however, because Section 1259 specifically cites them as causing constructive sales by being the perfect hedge. That means a collar must be used, and it can be put into effect using a variety of tools: options themselves, prepaid variable forward contracts, and swaps with embedded options.

The hedge must retain some risk of loss or potential for profit in the employee stock options. Although lawyers and accountants would like to know where to draw the line, there is no specific guidance, either in law or in IRS regulations, as to how much risk or reward must be retained to avoid running afoul of the constructive-sale rules.

For guidance, investment advisory firms such as Twenty-First Securities look to what is known as the "Blue Book," a publication of the Congressional Joint Committee on Taxation. The Blue Book's General Explanation of the Constructive Sale Rule uses the example of a 15-point spread, pointing toward the conclusion that a collar with a potential for losing 5 percent and a potential for earning 10 percent will not constitute a constructive sale. Both simple collars and forward sales offer an appropriate risk/reward band, and both, upon disposition, produce capital gains or losses rather than ordinary income or losses.

A simple collar involves buying a put with the strike price at or below the stock's current market price and simultaneously selling a call with a strike price at or above the current market price. The collar in effect establishes a floor below and a cap above the stock's current market price.

A forward sale involves a contract to sell stock at a specified future date. An investor can incorporate the economics of a collar into a forward contract by stipulating that the amount of stock to be delivered under the forward contract will vary depending upon the price of the stock on the expiration of the forward contract.

Both simple collars and forward sales can provide a tax-appropriate hedge and produce capital gains or losses when they are closed out.

Types of Employee Stock Options

THE HEDGE YOU CHOOSE TO USE depends in part on the kind of options you have. There are two kinds of employee stock options: qualified, or incentive, stock options and nonqualified stock options. When nonqualified options are exercised, the resulting income is treated as compensation income, or ordinary income, taxable at rates as high as 38.6 percent. In contrast, when qualified options are exercised, there is no current income. If the stock is held more than a year after exercise, the gain when it is sold or otherwise disposed of is treated as a long-term capital gain, taxable at a maximum rate of 20 percent.

Hedging Qualified Options

As noted above, both simple collars and forward sales provide a tax-appropriate hedge but produce capital gains or losses when they are closed out. Holders must remember to maintain a suitable level of risk in the arrangement.

Hedging Nonqualified Options

Hedging nonqualified options is somewhat more complicated than hedging qualified options. A key reason is that for holders of nonqualified options, if the shares continue to rise, collars

161

and forward sales can create a whipsaw: The holder could have both ordinary income on which he owes taxes and capital losses that are too large to be currently deductible. (Individual taxpayers can take only $3,000 of net capital losses per year against ordinary income; the balance must be carried forward to future years.)

The reason for the whipsaw is that income on nonqualified employee stock options is ordinary income, while income on regular (that is, qualified) stock options is capital in nature. So, for example, with a simple collar on nonqualified stock options, if the stock increases after the hedge is put on, then the investor will gain value on the employee stock options and lose value on the hedge position; these changes create more ordinary income—which is taxable at rates of up to 38.6 percent—on the options and corresponding capital losses on the hedge. Therefore, unless the option holder has short-term capital gains from other sources and thus can utilize the capital losses, this transaction would entail an after-tax loss of 38.6 cents for every $1 rise in the price of the stock.

The Swaps Solution for Hedging Nonqualified Options

FROM BOTH A TAX AND AN ECONOMIC perspective, swaps with embedded collars are a robust way to hedge nonqualified employee stock options. We recommend entering into a swap that incorporates options. For example, a former employee with options struck at 10 on stock that is now trading at 40 might do a swap with embedded options, such as a put struck at 38 and a call at 44. That means the option holder can buy stock that is worth four times as much as he would have to pay for it, a gain well worth protecting, especially in a volatile market. The embedded options in the swap would put a floor of two points under the current market price and a collar of four points above it, thus protecting nearly all the gain and allowing for a bit more appreciation before the holding would be called away.

Of course, a swap is viable only for substantial positions. Generally, there is a $3 million minimum on the transaction, and the option holder needs gross assets of $10 million to qualify. Assuming he or she does qualify, the participant enters into a contract with a swap dealer—generally a bank or security house. The participant agrees to make payment(s) to the dealer equal to the amount of any losses on the portfolio to a maximum of 5 percent and will receive any profits, to a maximum of 10 percent, plus an interest-based fee on the notional amount of the portfolio.

With a properly constructed swap, if the underlying stock continues to rise after the hedge has been put into place, then the swap itself should incur a corresponding loss that will be manifested through periodic payments made by the employee to the swap dealer. The IRS has ruled that all contractual payments made under a swap, including the final payment, must be treated as ordinary deductions (see Technical Advice Memorandum 97340007). That means the deductions can always be allocated against any further income on the employee stock options.

If the underlying stock should fall after the hedge is put on, then the swap should create a gain, so that the option holder does not share in the decline of the underlying stock. In a properly constructed swap, any movement in the stock price should be neutral, both in economics and in taxes, except as the collar allows.

Although swaps are probably the best way to hedge nonqualified employee stock options, there is a potential tax drawback: The ordinary deductions relating to swap payments are classified as "miscellaneous itemized deductions." Such deductions may be taken only to the extent that their total exceeds 2 percent of a taxpayer's adjusted gross income. A taxpayer who already has enough "other" itemized deductions to exceed the 2 percent floor is in an ideal position to enter into a swap contract. On the other hand, such deductions are disallowed for purposes of the alternative minimum tax. Therefore, an option holder should be cognizant of his income tax situation before entering into a swap contract.

Hedging Stock after Exercising Options

IN THE PAST, THERE HAS BEEN LITTLE that an employee who has exercised his options could do to protect the stock thus acquired during the year before it became a long-term holding. Recently, however, at least one specialized firm has offered to extend a loan for 90 percent of the stock's value. The stock is held in escrow, and if it rises after three years, the employee can repay the loan. If it falls, he can walk away from the stock and pay tax as if the stock were sold for that 90 percent.

The loans are available on securities worth as little as $100,000—considerably less than the minimum of $1 million or more that is frequently required in monetization strategies (for a discussion of monetization strategies, see Chapter 5). The loans carry interest rates of 10 percent to 12 percent, which is the cost of a put if purchased in the market without a loan. It sounds almost too good to be true, but the firm offering these nonrecourse loans claims that through the use of sophisticated mathematics it has developed financial engineering techniques that enable it to offer the loans.

Employees who have exercised their options are also allowed to sell call options on the stock they have purchased during the one-year period before it becomes a long-term holding, without stopping the clock on the holding period. These must be qualified covered calls, which at this writing are defined as listed options on which the strike price (the exercise price) can be no more than one strike price in the money—that is, it must not be too far from the market price. For example, if a stock is at $32, the holder can sell a call with a strike price above $30.

The combination of the nonrecourse loan and the calls can create the economics of a collar while still allowing the shares to age to long-term gains.

Other Regulatory Considerations

BECAUSE EMPLOYEE STOCK OPTIONS have no margin or collateral value, holders should be aware that a hedge usually requires appropriate margin or collateral from other sources. For large positions involving an issuer or employer who is cooperative, the options may be "converted" into a security that is publicly traded and thus is marginable. Unlike the "naked" options for which the holder does not own the underlying stock, a marginable security can be used to satisfy the requirement for collateral.

Holders of employee options should also be aware that "affiliates"—that is, people in a position to exercise substantial control over a company, such as directors, officers, or large stockholders—cannot sell short and can buy a put or sell a call only if they are long the same number of underlying shares. A holder of unexercised employee stock options is not generally considered to be long for these purposes.

ALTHOUGH THE TAX RULES ARE COMPLEX, they are well worth studying if you hold highly appreciated employee stock options. Knowing how to navigate the rules to construct an effective hedge can help you to protect holdings without incurring a tax liability, as you would by a direct sale.

CHAPTER 12

Avoiding Tax Traps for Closely Held Businesses

T HE FINANCIAL FOCUS OF MANY business owners, naturally, is on their business—so much so that tax concerns can fade into the distance—and that can lead to tax problems. In this chapter we look at some of the popular forms of business organization for closely held businesses (that is, businesses owned by only a few shareholders, the shares of which are not available to outside buyers) and the tax traps that can ensnare their owners. We then discuss how to avoid those traps—and what to do if you have accidentally sprung them.

Personal Holding Companies

AS INNOCUOUS AS THE NAME may sound, a personal holding company is a tax trap, so our first piece of advice is: Avoid it. Unfortunately, the first time many people hear of a personal holding company is after they have been caught in the trap, so the problem is how to get out of it.

When corporate tax rates were significantly lower than individual rates, Congress developed the concept of the personal holding company to prevent individuals from forming corporations as vehicles for making personal investments and thus getting more favorable tax treatment than they would as individuals. In 1980, for example, when the top individual rate was 70 percent, the top corporate rate was 46 percent. So suppose an individual owed $100,000 in taxes on investment income. If he could instead pay taxes at the corporate rate, he would owe only $65,714—a tax savings of $34,286.

Although the rate structures and other aspects of the tax code have changed substantially in the past two decades, the personal holding company rules remain intact. Today, PHCs, as they are known, in addition to being subject to the prevailing corporate tax rules, must also pay a 38.6 percent tax on any undistributed personal holding company income, so that income is taxed as if it had been distributed.

Section 542 of the Internal Revenue Code gives two essential criteria for a personal holding company. A corporation is considered a PHC if:

1 At any time in the second half of the year more than half the stock is owned by five or fewer individuals (there are certain legal exceptions: organizations, as described in Sections 401(a), 501(c)(17), or 509(a), or a portion of certain trusts, as described in Section 642(c), may be considered individuals); and

2 It derives at least 60 percent of its adjusted ordinary gross income from any of the following sources described in Section 543:
   ❑ interest and dividends
   ❑ produced film rentals

❑ royalties from minerals, oil, and gas

❑ copyright royalties

❑ income received for the use of corporate property by a shareholder who owns 25 percent or more of the company's stock

❑ personal service contracts

❑ certain income from estates and trusts

How Asset Sales May Spring the Trap

A common way that people inadvertently spring the PHC trap is by selling the assets of a closely held business to a large corporation and accepting the corporation's stock as payment for the assets of their business. Say, for example, the owners of the Smith Widget Company want to sell their business and retire to Florida. Some big companies are interested—but only in the assets of Smith Widget, not in the company itself, because the purchasing company can depreciate the assets. So the owners of Smith Widget strike a deal in which Giant Company gets all Smith Widget's assets and Smith Widget receives Giant stock rather than cash. The Smith Widget owners then own a corporate shell that owns stock in Giant Company. That stock is the primary source of their corporation's income, which means the Smith Widget owners could have a personal holding company—and face the liability of double taxation.

If they restructure the business to have just one level of tax, by electing S corporation status or converting to a limited liability company, for example, the restructuring itself is likely to lead to a big tax liability. Their goal is to keep the present corporation and make enough of its investments produce "good income" (in other words, income from sources other than those listed above) so that it will not be considered a PHC.

People who find they own a PHC that has cash to invest often buy tax-exempt securities, because the interest paid by tax-exempts such as munis is not included in ordinary adjusted gross income. This tactic avoids exacerbating the problem, but it does not reduce the percentage of PHC income in ordinary adjusted gross income from other sources.

How to Free Yourself from the Trap

If you find yourself in this situation, your goal should be to create "good" income in place of "bad" income, like interest. If you can move enough of the corporation's interest-bearing holdings into assets that instead produce ordinary income from any source other than those listed above from Section 543, you can solve the problem. Another way to solve it is to take the money out of an interest-bearing account or investment and put it into a hedged investment. For example, you could buy gold and hedge the holding with gold futures or buy SPDRs (investment trust securities that mimic the movements of the Standard & Poor's 500 index) and hedge them with an options contract on the S&P 500. The transactions are safe because they are hedged, and, importantly, they produce conversion income, which is good for this purpose.

Remember the conversion rules discussed in Chapter 3, "Techniques for Utilizing Your Losses?" There an investor wanted to avoid conversion income, but in this situation, you are deliberately failing the conversion-income test, because conversion transactions have great benefits for PHCs, simply because conversion income is not PHC income, so you can avoid double taxation.

By way of a refresher, the IRS defines a conversion transaction as any transaction that you entered into after April 30, 1993, that fulfills both of these criteria:

1 Substantially all of your expected return from the transaction is due to the time value of your net investment, and

2 The transaction is one of the following:

❑ a straddle, including any set of offsetting positions on stock;

❑ any transaction in which you acquire property (whether or not actively traded) at substantially the same time that you contract to sell the same property or substantially identical property at a price set in the contract; or

❑ any other transaction that is marketed or sold as producing capital gains from a transaction described in the first test.

So investing in a totally hedged transaction should produce an interest-based return that purposely fails the tests of the conversion rules, thereby creating "good," noninterest income for the PHC.

Master Limited Partnerships

Another way to garner good income is to invest in master limited partnerships. These securities are listed on the New York and American stock exchanges, where they trade like any other stock, but they are treated as partnerships for tax purposes so a proportionate share of the partnership's gross income flows through to its investors. (It should be noted that it is the gross revenue of the entity and not its net income that flows through.) Because they are listed, they are readily available and have good liquidity. Among the partnerships are Amerigas Partners-L.P., Borden Chemicals and Plastic UT, El Paso Energy Partners L.P., Eott Energy Partners-L.P., Ferrell Gas Partners-L.P., Genesis Energy L.P., Phosphate Resources

Partners, Plains All American Pipeline L.P., Suburban Propane Partners L.P., Star Gas Partners L.P., and Teppco Partners-L.P.

But for the purposes of creating "good" income for a closely held business, do not buy just any partnership. Many of those mentioned above are in the energy business; if their income is from oil and gas royalties, for example, they would not produce "good income" for PHC purposes, but if their income is from energy transport, as is the case for many of them, it would be "good income" for PHC purposes. And importantly, the partnership chosen should operate a business for which the level of gross receipts is high compared to the investment needed to buy the interest. For example, in February 2001, Borden Chemicals and Plastic offered revenues of $17.58 per dollar invested, while Plains All American Pipeline L.P. offered $6.43 per dollar invested. Even after making the investment, it is important to monitor it carefully because the company's gross income can change, so you may want to sell shares of one partnership and buy those of another.

Investors may also want to consider hedging the partnership investment to remove risk from the holding.

S Corporations

SUBCHAPTER S CORPORATIONS are a popular form of organization for closely held businesses because they provide corporate protection while passing through income to be taxed only on the personal level, thus avoiding the double taxation of dividends (at both the corporate and shareholder level) that occurs for regular, or C, corporations. But tax traps can ensnare S-corporation shareholders who are not alert to the tax rules.

The Passive Activity Trap

If an S corporation derives more than 25 percent of its gross receipts from passive investment income and has also accumulated earnings and profits in the same year, the corporation may be subject to a corporate level of tax. If the company meets this 25 percent threshold for three consecutive years and has accumulated earnings and profits for each of those years, it will lose its S corporation status.

The IRS defines a passive activity as one involving the conduct of a trade or business in which you do not materially participate, and most rental activities. However, the rental of real estate is not a passive activity if both of the following are true:

1 More than one-half of the personal services you perform during the year in all trades or businesses are performed in real property trades or businesses in which you materially participate; and
2 You perform more than 750 hours of services during the year in real property trades or businesses in which you materially participate.

Buying Partnership Units to Avoid Passive Income

An S corporation that faces the passive-income problem described above could also solve it by purchasing an interest in a publicly traded master limited partnership, as described in the preceding section. If the partnership investment is leveraged—that is, purchased on margin—the S corporation could get even more "good" income for its investment. As a partner, the corporation will include its share of the partnership's gross receipts for purposes of the 25 percent test.

A specialized brokerage firm can assist the S corporation in entering into hedging transactions to reduce the economic exposure inherent in the partnership investment. The risk-reduction techniques ought not have an effect on the gross receipts test. Thus, again, a fully hedged transaction yielding money-market rates can solve a seemingly unconnected tax issue.

Limited Liability Companies

LIMITED LIABILITY COMPANIES, or LLCs as they are generally known, have become popular in recent years. Like S corporations or general or limited partnerships, they are flow-through entities (that is, tax is due only at the personal level, not at the corporate level, and income and deductions are allocated to the owners). In terms of tax, LLCs are thus on a par with S corporations and general partnerships, but they have an important nontax advantage over those other forms of business organization: In an LLC, the owners can manage the business without subjecting themselves to personal liability.

Another advantage is that like a corporation with different classes of stock, each LLC ownership interest may have various management, voting, and distribution characteristics. That can provide a business owner with a way to shift income to a child or family member while retaining control and voting rights of the business.

Still, it is easy to run afoul of the tax laws in converting a family business to an LLC. Partnerships may convert to the LLC form with no tax consequences, but a C or S corporation may not convert to the LLC form unless the corporation goes through an actual liquidation or a deemed liquidation for tax purposes. Further, there are questions as to which members of an LLC may be subject to self-employment tax, and because LLCs are authorized under federal law but organized under state law, different statutes in different states add another level of complexity. Business owners, therefore, should consult a local tax expert before converting a business to an LLC.

Family Partnerships

ONE ALTERNATIVE FORM OF BUSINESS organization for a family-owned business is a family limited partnership, or FLP. The partnership offers a valuable tax-planning opportunity: An owner can make a gift of a minority interest in her business to her children or other heirs and discount the value of the interest because it is a minority interest without control and because it lacks marketability. Under the 2001 tax law, gift taxes remain in existence, but estate taxes are to end in the year 2010. For the years 2002 through 2009, the amount that can be excluded from taxable estates is to rise gradually from $1 million to $3.5 million. Unless another law is passed, as would seem likely, estate taxes would resume in 2011. Given this fluid situation, business owners generally need to consult a lawyer who specializes in trusts and estates to be sure their gifting and estate plans are up-to-date, and in particular anyone considering giving a minority interest needs to do so.

FLPs are also flow-through entities, so that all FLP income is taxed directly to the individual partners. If you give shares to your children and they are not in the highest tax bracket, the FLP may offer income tax savings, especially in comparison with setting up a trust. Generally, taxes on trusts are higher than taxes on individuals with the same income, because the top rate of 39.1 percent in 2001, for example, takes effect at only $8,900 for trusts. Furthermore, an FLP agreement can be modified, whereas a trust agreement generally cannot be, and the "business judgment rule" that applies to managing partners is generally less strict than the "prudent man rule" that applies to trustees. To be sure that the FLP is recognized for both state law and tax purposes, a business owner should get expert legal and tax advice in the state where it operates.

AS APPEALING AS OWNING A BUSINESS may be, it can be much more rewarding if you choose the best form of organization for your particular business and its tax situation, especially if you might sell the business one day and accept stock in the acquiring corporation as payment. Should you spring the personal-holding-company trap, you can rectify the situation by using one of the strategies described in this chapter, but, of course, it is better to avoid springing it, and choosing the right form of organization and the right investments for "good income" should help you do that.

CHAPTER 13

Planning for
Often-Overlooked
State Taxes

OFTEN TAXPAYERS FOCUS on keeping the IRS from eating their lunch only to discover that state tax authorities have taken a huge bite. State taxes accounted for an astounding 45 percent of all corporate taxes paid in the United States, a study by Coopers & Lybrand found in 1993.

Why? There is no simple explanation. No state levies income taxes at a rate nearly as high as that 45 percent figure would indicate, but each of the fifty states and the District of Columbia has its own set of tax laws, and not only for income taxes but also for property, sales, excise, estate, and other taxes as the table on state tax collections at the end of this chapter shows. Furthermore, the percentage of state revenue from each type of tax varies widely among the states. Florida, for example, gets 58.3 percent of its tax revenue from general sales and use taxes but levies no personal or corporate income tax; New Hampshire, in contrast, collects no sales and use tax, but gets 5.9 percent of its tax revenues from individual income taxes and 23.9

percent from corporate income taxes. The Tax Foundation, a Washington-based research organization, says that state and local taxes took 10.4 percent of Americans' income in the year 2000, while the total tax burden, including federal taxes, took 33.3 percent.

Reducing the state tax bite to a negligible nibble depends not only on the particular state in which you live or do business but also on the nature of your income and, if you own your own business, the type of business you are in—whether you have a large plant in a location with high property taxes, inventories that may be taxable, a start-up business with net operating losses (which some states treat more leniently than others), a fleet of vehicles, and myriad other factors.

Given the complexity of all the state laws, this chapter cannot possibly be comprehensive. What we hope to do is alert you to the issues and encourage anyone contemplating a personal move or business relocation to ask his or her accountant to check into the precise effects of the particular move before making a final decision. You do not, after all, want to be like the surgeon who upon retirement sold his home in New York, a high-tax state, and moved to New Hampshire, which he believed did not levy an income tax, only to discover that while there was no state income tax on earned income (which he no longer had), as a result of the state taxes on the dividends and interest on which he lived, he did not live state-tax-free. Similarly, Florida has no income tax, but it imposes an intangibles tax on investments. So while its weather may beckon to retirees, its tax laws, while favorable, leave a slight cloud on the horizon.

We also cite examples of some state tax strategies that investors and business owners have used successfully.

Understanding the Variations among State Taxes

IF YOU WANT TO HOLD ONTO as much of your money as possible, move to Wyoming, *Bloomberg Personal Finance* magazine has advised. The magazine performed an exhaustive analysis of the taxes that four hypothetical families in each state and the District of Columbia would have owed and reported the results of its study in May 2001. It measured not only income taxes but also real estate and sales taxes. The table on pages 180–182 ranks the states numerically for both overall wealth-friendliness and for retirement and gives each a report-card-style grade.

Wyoming, the winner, received an A+, finishing first in both categories. The loser was Rhode Island, which landed in the 51st spot in both categories; its grade was F. But Rhode Island was not far behind its Northeastern neighbors. New York was No. 49 overall, Maine 48, Vermont 45, and the District of Columbia 43.

Joining Wyoming in the top ten wealth-friendly states overall were: Tennessee, Nevada, Washington, Alaska, Florida, South Dakota, Louisiana, Alabama, and Texas.

Steve Gittelson, the magazine's editor, noted that "there's more to life than taxes," but, he added, wealth-friendliness could be a factor in deciding where to live, especially as tele-commuting allows more people to work wherever they choose.

Montanans, for example, might want to move over the state line to Wyoming. Their state ranked 50th overall and 49th for retirement and was graded D-. The other states in the bottom ten overall were: Nebraska 42, Minnesota 44, Oregon 46, and Wisconsin 47. Nor was the Wyoming-Montana disparity the only one between neighbors. Next to 46th-ranked Oregon is

179

Ranking the States by Wealth Friendliness

State	Overall Grade	Overall Rank	Retirement Rank
Alabama	B+	9	7
Alaska	A	5	9
Arizona	B	14	12
Arkansas	C	31	17
California	C-	39	15
Colorado	B	12	18
Connecticut	C-	38	42
Delaware	B	11	6
District of Columbia	D+	43	29
Florida	A	6	8
Georgia	C	27	28
Hawaii	C	30	14
Idaho	C-	41	38
Illinois	C	28	31
Indiana	B-	17	21
Iowa	C	36	33
Kansas	C-	37	44

State	Overall Grade	Overall Rank	Retirement Rank
Kentucky	C	35	13
Louisiana	A-	8	2
Maine	D	48	43
Maryland	C+	18	22
Massachusetts	C	32	30
Michigan	C+	24	34
Minnesota	D+	44	48
Mississippi	C+	20	10
Missouri	C+	25	39
Montana	D-	50	49
Nebraska	D+	42	47
Nevada	A	3	5
New Hampshire	B	13	37
New Jersey	C	34	32
New Mexico	C+	21	35
New York	D	49	45
North Carolina	C-	40	16

(continued on the following page)

Ranking the States by Wealth Friendliness
(continued)

State	Overall Grade	Overall Rank	Retirement Rank
North Dakota	B-	16	36
Ohio	C	26	20
Oklahoma	C	33	27
Oregon	D+	46	40
Pennsylvania	C+	19	23
Rhode Island	F	51	51
South Carolina	C	29	19
South Dakota	A	7	11
Tennessee	A+	2	3
Texas	B	10	25
Utah	B-	15	26
Vermont	D+	45	46
Virginia	C+	22	24
Washington	A	4	4
West Virginia	C+	23	41
Wisconsin	D	47	50
Wyoming	A+	1	1

Source: *Bloomberg Personal Finance*

4th-ranked Washington; California ranked 39th, while neighboring Nevada was 3rd; and Maryland, 18th, adjoins the District of Columbia, 43rd. One surprise in the survey: Massachusetts is shedding its Taxachusetts moniker and now ranks 32rd overall and 30th for retirement. Still, its grade is only C.

Of particular interest to investors, perhaps, are the retirement ratings, as they were based in large part on how the states taxed investment income. The results of the magazine's study are a good starting point for people who may be relocating and want to consider the tax impact of a move. But they are averages, so it is still important to get advice about your individual situation. (After all, no matter what the national average may be, who do you know who has 1.7 children?)

Some states, for example, have graduated tax rates—Idaho has eight rates ranging from 1.9 percent to 8.1 percent—while others have a single rate. Massachusetts's rate is 5.85 percent. Rhode Island's income tax is 26 percent of a taxpayer's federal income tax liability.

Financing the Purchase of Treasury Bonds

SIX STATES—ALABAMA, COLORADO, Illinois, Maryland, North Dakota, and Vermont—do not currently tax interest income from U.S. Treasury obligations but do allow taxpayers to take deductions for expenses incurred in connection with the purchase and financing of those securities, including interest expenses and amortization of bond premiums. Taxpayers in these states who expect interest rates to drop can take advantage of these rules by making a highly leveraged purchase of a Treasury obligation that will mature shortly. The degree of leverage is negotiable, but on a thirty-year bond, the investor might put up 10 percent. If interest rates decline, the investor should make a profit on the transaction. In addition, because interest income from Treasuries is free of state taxes in those six states and the investor can claim a state tax deduction for the interest expense, the investor may be able to earn an after-tax profit even if interest rates do not decline, thereby wiping out the taxpayer's state tax liability.

Caveats on Buying Municipal Bonds

THE STATE TAX ADVANTAGE that most often occurs to investors is to buy municipal bonds issued by their own state. An in-state bond is free of state taxes, as well as federal taxes. In New York City, which taxes residents' incomes, local municipal bonds are triple-tax-free. But a word of caution is in order: When there is high demand for a security, the issuer can market it successfully with a low coupon. Run the numbers. You may be better off with an out-of-state security that offers a higher yield. A New York City resident might do better buying a bond issued by Virginia or Texas, for example. An alternative for residents of any state is Puerto Rican debt securities, for they are treated like in-state securities, being exempt from both federal and state taxes.

A final caution: Investigate credit quality before buying a bond. Tax minimization should be secondary to sound investment criteria in deciding where to put your money.

Reducing Corporate Taxes

THE ISSUE OF STATE TAXES may be more important to business owners than to employees, because there are more variables that could affect an entrepreneur's decision on where to incorporate or operate a business than there are for individual taxpayers.

A rate table alone does not tell the story. Arthur Gelber, a certified public accountant who specializes in state taxes, was quoted in *The New York Times* as having said, "You might have a high-rate state but wind up with a low effective rate with proper planning."[2] For example, he once convinced a client to move his business into New York. Despite relatively high corporate income tax brackets, in many ways New York's tax structure is friendlier to business than that of many other states, Gelber said.

In the case he mentioned, the client was in the investment business. New York, thanks to its Wall Street history, ranks along with Delaware and Nevada as the most favorable locations for minimizing tax on intangible investment income, such as interest and dividends. New York is also relatively hospitable for businesses that sell large volumes of goods out of state, because it allows businesses to use an allocation formula, so that income is taxed where it is earned, not all in the headquarters state. California, in contrast, uses a unitary formula, under which it attempts to tax worldwide income from activities of any related companies in other states or countries.

Other variables that Gelber cited include the following:

❑ **Net operating losses**. Some states, including Massachusetts, Connecticut, and Pennsylvania, do not conform to federal net operating loss provisions. Rather, they limit tax-loss carryforwards. That may impose a burden on start-up businesses, which typically lose money in their early years but hope to deduct those losses from future profits for tax purposes.

❑ **Real estate taxes.** These vary considerably, but in some areas they can take a big bite out of the profits of a business with a large plant.

❑ **Incentives.** Some jurisdictions have economic development zones that either offer businesses reduced sales tax or real estate taxes to locate there or offer employers income tax credits for hiring people in areas of high unemployment, like the South Bronx in New York City.

❑ **Other taxes.** There are a wide variety of other taxes that can trip up the unwary. For example, Texas does not have an income tax, but it has a levy on a business's capital base. Los Angeles County has a gross receipts tax, and Georgia taxes inventories.

Some Strategies That Have Worked

HERE ARE EXAMPLES OF corporate tax-planning strategies available in New York and New Jersey. Doubtless, similar techniques could be used in other states after careful research of state laws.

Reducing New York's Franchise Tax

Under the New York State and New York City rules on the taxation of investment income, a bond that has less than six months to maturity is treated as cash. Unless a taxpayer has other investment income, the interest received on cash or cash equivalents is allocated according to the taxpayer's business allocation.

Therefore, if a corporation—say, New York Manufacturing—uses excess cash to buy short-term debt instruments and has no other investments, the income earned on those instruments is allocated to New York based upon New York Manufacturing's business allocation percentage. However, if New York Manufacturing purchases the securities of another corporation, such as AMR, which has a lower (or zero) allocation percentage in New York, then New York Manufacturing can capture returns that New York will tax based on AMR's allocation. Because AMR has zero allocation in New York, the AMR profit will not be subject to taxes in New York. If a sufficient amount of New York Manufacturing's excess cash is invested in the securities of such zero-allocation corporations, then New York Manufacturing may be able to convert all its interest income into state-tax-free investment income. Even cash investments with maturities of less than six months could be converted into such tax-free investment income.

Of course, to achieve this tax-free result, you would have had to purchase equities instead of the less volatile bonds you wanted. Therefore, because the ownership of corporate stock always entails risks, you ought to combine your stock purchase with an appropriate derivatives-based hedge. That way, you can, in effect, turn your corporate shares into the equivalent of a Treasury bill that will qualify for the favorable allocation rules.

Selling Tax Losses in New Jersey

The New Jersey Emerging Technology and Biotechnology Financial Assistance Act provides important tax-planning opportunities for New Jersey companies. The act allows technology and biotechnology companies to surrender unused tax benefits for tax years beginning on or after January 1, 1999, in exchange for private financial assistance.

Qualifying companies may petition the Department of Revenue for permission to sell unused research and development credits or unused net operating losses (NOLs) for a minimum of 75 percent of the surrendered tax benefit. The purchasing corporation may then use the NOL or apply the credit on its New Jersey tax return.

Say a company—NJ Technology—has an NOL of $1 million. It can sell that NOL to another New Jersey corporate taxpayer for 75 percent of the tax benefit and receive immediately available financial assistance of $67,500 (that is, 75 percent of the tax benefit on $1 million at a tax rate of 9 percent). The purchasing corporation receives an immediate tax savings of $22,500 (that is, the remaining 25 percent of the tax benefit). Thus, the program encourages two types of companies to remain in-state: technology companies, which can realize some money from their tax losses, and profitable companies, which can reduce their tax expenses by as much as 25 percent.

One notable aspect of this program is that any corporation purchasing these tax benefits is virtually immune from any adjustments made by the New Jersey tax authorities on audit. Any audit adjustments are borne by the selling company, not the purchasing company.

The favorable response to the program has been overwhelming. In the first six months of 1999, the act drew far more potential sale transactions than was expected when the legislation was enacted in 1998. Indeed, the surge of interest prompted legislators to worry about revenue. As a result, the legislature delayed implementing the act until it had modified it.

The modified act caps the revenue cost to New Jersey in the first three years of the program at $130 million. With a 9 percent New Jersey corporate tax rate, more than $1.4 billion of tax-loss carryforwards and tax-credit carryforwards could have been sold.

Organizing as an LLC

Limited liability companies, or LLCs, permit corporations to reduce not only federal but also state taxes. In terms of risk protection, LLCs are like corporations because they can enter into contracts and protect investors from company debt. In terms of taxes, however, they are like partnerships: Income flows through to investors directly instead of being taxed at the business-entity level. This combination of corporation and partnership features makes the LLC a great way to do business. What's more, the tax treatment of LLCs gives rise to several hidden state income tax opportunities.

One such opportunity involves state income tax nexus. Usually the revenue a corporation generates in-state is subject to state income tax. Many states, however, do not tax LLCs separately; instead they tax an LLC's shareholders. Out-of-state shareholders are sometimes exempt from these taxes. It follows that it may be possible in certain states to transfer an LLC's taxable income to out-of-state shareholders and thus avoid state income tax altogether. Businesses considering this approach should examine specific state tax laws. In some states, if a corporation actively manages an LLC in-state, it will be deemed to be doing business in that state and will therefore be subject to state tax. A corporation can sometimes avoid this result by delegating the management of an LLC to a subsidiary. A corporation in one state that merely invests in an LLC in another state is often not subject to income taxes in the state where the LLC operates.

An additional break may be available to start-up LLCs. Start-ups usually generate losses in their early years. When a corporation is profitable and its start-up subsidiary creates

189

State Tax Collections and Distributions by Type of Tax, Fiscal Year 1999

	Total ($Thousands)	DISTRIBUTION	
		General Sales & Use	Individual Income
All States (*)	$499,510,046	33.20%	34.50%
Alabama	$6,032,234	27.30	31.60
Alaska	905,135	0.00	0.00
Arizona	7,542,735	43.90	27.80
Arkansas	4,608,936	34.80	31.10
California	72,387,698	31.30	42.50
Colorado	5,987,125	28.50	46.90
Connecticut	9,623,591	33.40	37.50
Delaware	2,030,789	0.00	38.00
District of Columbia†	2,932,814	19.90	31.20
Florida	23,791,570	58.30	0.00
Georgia	12,461,790	34.90	45.70
Hawaii	3,166,663	45.70	33.80
Idaho	2,171,127	32.30	39.00
Illinois	21,211,263	28.00	34.20
Indiana	9,736,077	34.00	38.00

Corporate Income	Motor Fuels	Licenses	All Other
6.10%	5.80%	6.10%	14.20%
3.90	8.20	7.50	21.40
23.40	4.20	9.40	63.00
7.20	7.80	3.30	10.00
4.60	8.20	4.70	16.50
7.50	4.20	4.30	10.20
5.00	8.60	4.90	6.10
4.90	5.70	3.80	14.70
11.50	5.10	33.30	12.20
6.80	1.00	1.70	39.30
5.30	6.60	6.30	23.40
6.40	4.50	3.40	5.10
1.70	2.30	3.00	13.60
4.40	9.80	9.40	5.00
9.90	6.30	5.90	15.70
10.20	6.80	2.20	8.80

(continued on the following page)

State Tax Collections and Distributions
by Type of Tax, Fiscal Year 1999 *(continued)*

		DISTRIBUTION	
	Total ($Thousands)	General Sales & Use	Individual Income
Iowa	$4,868,494	33.80%	35.20%
Kansas	4,589,475	36.70	37.00
Kentucky	7,355,861	28.40	34.40
Louisiana	6,029,883	37.60	25.50
Maine	2,540,581	32.60	40.10
Maryland	9,479,949	24.30	44.10
Massachusetts	14,731,769	22.20	54.60
Michigan	23,334,348	35.60	31.70
Minnesota	12,481,688	27.30	42.50
Mississippi	$4,573,825	48.80	21.50
Missouri	8,563,594	31.70	42.40
Montana	1,365,304	0.00	35.40
Nebraska	2,662,103	32.10	40.30
Nevada	3,430,007	53.30	0.00
New Hampshire	1,070,803	0.00	5.90
New Jersey	16,926,421	29.90	37.40

Corporate Income	Motor Fuels	Licenses	All Other
4.80%	7.00%	9.60%	9.50%
5.50	7.10	5.10	8.60
4.20	6.00	6.60	20.30
4.70	8.90	8.40	14.90
5.80	6.80	4.90	9.70
4.30	7.20	3.80	16.40
8.50	4.30	2.90	7.50
10.10	4.70	5.00	13.00
6.20	4.70	7.00	12.30
5.00	8.60	6.20	9.90
3.20	7.70	7.00	7.90
6.60	13.20	8.60	36.30
5.10	9.90	6.50	6.10
0.00	6.90	10.00	29.70
23.90	11.20	12.40	46.70
7.90	2.90	4.50	17.60

(continued on the following page)

193

State Tax Collections and Distributions
by Type of Tax, Fiscal Year 1999 *(continued)*

	Total ($Thousands)	DISTRIBUTION	
		General Sales & Use	Individual Income
New Mexico	$3,484,206	41.70%	23.20%
New York	38,700,773	20.60	53.20
North Carolina	14,436,294	23.20	45.60
North Dakota	1,106,499	30.10	16.40
Ohio	18,175,451	32.30	39.60
Oklahoma	5,417,232	25.40	38.20
Oregon	5,341,403	0.00	69.40
Pennsylvania	21,588,754	30.80	29.70
Rhode Island	1,895,196	29.60	40.20
South Carolina	$5,823,476	40.30	34.10
South Dakota	868,211	53.20	0.00
Tennessee	7,191,307	58.60	2.20
Texas	25,675,587	51.00	0.00
Utah	3,644,467	37.80	40.10
Vermont	1,011,616	20.30	37.90
Virginia	11,562,735	20.70	52.70

Corporate Income	Motor Fuels	Licenses	All Other
4.70%	7.10%	5.60%	17.70%
7.50	1.30	2.40	15.10
6.40	7.90	6.10	10.90
8.50	9.50	7.60	28.00
4.10	7.50	7.60	8.90
3.50	7.10	13.90	12.00
6.10	7.40	9.80	7.20
7.10	3.50	10.70	18.20
3.50	6.30	4.70	15.60
4.00	6.00	7.30	8.30
5.80	12.40	12.40	16.30
7.90	10.70	9.50	11.10
0.00	10.10	14.50	24.40
4.90	8.60	3.70	5.00
4.90	5.60	6.50	24.80
3.60	6.90	4.20	12.00

(continued on the following page)

195

State Tax Collections and Distributions
by Type of Tax, Fiscal Year 1999 *(continued)*

		DISTRIBUTION	
	Total ($Thousands)	General Sales and Use	Individual Income
Washington	$12,337,555	58.80%	0.00%
West Virginia	3,148,108	28.50	29.20
Wisconsin	11,627,782	28.10	44.40
Wyoming	812,556	42.80	0.00

(*) Does not include District of Columbia

† Quarterly Data

losses, the corporation may choose to file a consolidated return for federal and state tax purposes. With a consolidated return, it can use the start-up's losses to offset its income. However, state rules regarding consolidated tax returns vary greatly. Some states never allow separate businesses to file consolidated returns, and others impose tight restrictions on the practice. Because LLCs are not taxed as corporations, however, it may be possible to avoid this problem. For example, by choosing flow-through LLC status, a new venture should be able to apply its losses against the income of its profitable parent. This would give the parent the same tax result as if it filed a consolidated tax return with its subsidiary.

Corporate Income	Motor Fuels	Licenses	All Other
0.00%	5.80%	4.60%	30.80%
8.40	7.50	5.10	21.30
5.80	7.80	5.70	8.30
0.00	7.70	10.10	39.50

Source: Tax Foundation, based on data from the Department of Commerce, Bureau of the Census.

THE KEY TO MANAGING STATE TAXES is individual analysis of state tax laws. State laws on LLCs are complex and subject to change, but they are still worth the effort it takes to master them. The state corporate tax burden is substantial, and the breaks available to limited liability companies, for example, are significant. So, pack your bags, move to Laramie, and set up your business as an LLC—unless, of course, you might find life without the Metropolitan Museum of Art unbearable.

PART 4

Your
Annual
Opportunity

CHAPTER 14

Year-End
Planning Strategies

ALTHOUGH WE HAVE EMPHASIZED that loss harvesting and other tax-saving strategies ought to be a year-round discipline (see Chapter 2), not only year-end activities, we certainly have not meant to imply that year-end tax planning can be neglected. On the contrary, for tax-efficient investing it is vital to review your portfolio in the fourth quarter and take whatever actions are appropriate to reduce or defer taxes—in fact, some tax-saving opportunities are available *only* toward the end of the year.

Either sit down with your tax adviser and go over your income, investments, and deductions for the current year, or use TurboTax or TaxCut to run the numbers on your computer. Even if you have a CPA prepare your return, the software, which is quite inexpensive, can be a great help in getting organized and exploring options during the fourth quarter.

Assess Your Liability for the Alternative Minimum Tax

A KEY TAX-PLANNING QUESTION IS, are you going to be liable for the alternative minimum tax? The rates are lower than they are for the regular tax system—the top bracket is still 28 percent versus 38.6 percent for the regular system until 2004—but far fewer tax breaks are allowed, so the resultant tax can be higher.

In essence, although the tax code allows a wide variety of deductions, credits, and preferential treatments, overall it is more like a menu from a Chinese restaurant (Choose one from Column A and one from Column B) than like a smorgasbord that lets you take as much as you want. People who avail themselves of too many breaks under the regular system—say, deducting state and local taxes, exercising incentive stock options, claiming depreciation or depletion, investing in certain private-purpose municipal bonds, or reporting that a substantial part of their income comes from long-term capital gains—may find themselves tripped up by the alternative minimum tax (AMT). Under the tax code you are liable for whichever tax is higher, regular or AMT. Heads, the IRS wins; tails, you lose.

What is more, the accounting firm Deloitte & Touche has warned in a booklet, "Seeds of Change, the 2001 Tax Cut," that "many families will likely be shocked to find that the Act, for the first time, pulls them into the AMT," largely because of the narrowing of the rate differences between regular and AMT rates.

Using the example of a couple with two children and $150,000 in income on which they would previously have owed $24,500 in taxes, the firm projected the couple would get a $2,800 tax cut, once the act is fully effective, but said that were there no AMT, their taxes would have been cut an additional $700. "So while the couple still gets a cut under the Act, it's smaller because of AMT, plus they must deal with added complexity," the firm wrote.

Indeed, the staff of the Joint Committee on Taxation estimates that 35.5 million individual tax returns, or nearly a quarter of those filed, will have an AMT liability by 2010. That is more than twenty-five times the 1.4 million expected for 2001 and contrasts sharply with 140,000, or one-tenth of 1 percent of the individual returns, that had an AMT liability in 1987. The Joint Committee staff has recommended that the AMT be eliminated, but so far Congress has not acted on that recommendation.

Given the trend of the AMT to sweep ever more taxpayers into its net, it is more important than ever to determine in the fourth quarter whether you may be liable for the AMT. If so, you may choose to defer exercising some or all of the incentive stock options you hold, for example, or avoid realizing too many capital gains or investing in certain municipal bonds or bond funds that would be taxable for AMT purposes. The AMT rules are extremely complicated, and we cannot emphasize strongly enough that if you may be liable for it you should get professional tax advice. (The AMT also raises noninvestment issues, such as whether to pay fourth-quarter estimated state taxes or real estate taxes before or after year-end, but we will not go into them here.)

An idea that would be appropriate if you are in an AMT situation is to accelerate income into the current year, raising the regular tax up to the AMT level—a move that creates no new taxes. For example, you might cash in a Series EE bond. Another idea would be to enter in a leveraged transaction that realizes income this year but incurs interest expense that could be deductible next year when your rate could be as high as 38.6 percent.

Projected AMT Liabilities through 2010

During the decade 2001 through 2010 the number of taxpayers liable for the alternative minimum tax is expected to surge. Nearly a quarter of the returns filed are projected to have an AMT liability at the end of the decade, a number that has increased greatly as a result of the 2001 tax law, which narrowed the gap between AMT tax rates and regular rates.

Returns with AMT Liabilities

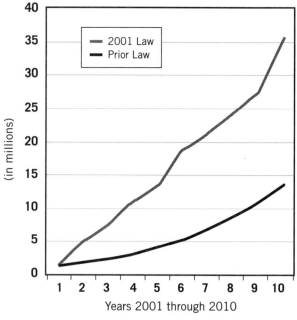

Source: Joint Committee on Taxation

Review Your Stock and Bond Portfolios

STUDIES HAVE SHOWN THAT INVESTORS tend to sell winners in their portfolios and hold losers in the hope that the losers will come back at least to the price at which they bought them. This perhaps reflects a psychological tendency to avoid admitting an error. But for both maximum investment performance and tax efficiency it is better to sell a portfolio's losers—using the losses to offset short-term gains and ordinary income, when possible—and hold the long-term winners. (For more detail on this, review Chapter 2, on loss harvesting.)

The reason capital losses are most useful when applied against ordinary income or short-term gains is that they provide a dollar-for-dollar offset to income that would otherwise be taxed at rates of up to 38.6 percent. If losses offset long-term capital gains (for securities, more than one year), they are offsetting income that would be taxed at a maximum rate of 20 percent.

Under the tax code, you must take short-term losses first against short-term gains, and then take long-term losses against long-term gains. Finally, you can take the net short-term gain or loss against the net long-term gain or loss. If that results in a net capital loss, you can take up to $3,000 a year against ordinary income, such as salaries, dividends, or interest. Losses in excess of $3,000 can generally be carried forward to future years to be taken first against capital gains and then against ordinary income (with the same $3,000 annual limit).

Avoid Wash Sales

Portfolios with paper losses do not always have paper gains that neatly offset them, and often investors still have faith in a holding that is under water. So the problem becomes how to recognize the loss for tax purposes but to keep the holding. That is possible, but investors must be mindful of the "wash sale" rules in Section 1091 of the Internal Revenue Code, which mandate that the loss cannot be recognized for tax purposes if the same or substantially identical new shares are purchased within thirty days of recognizing the loss. Because of various revisions, the wash-sale rules include among the affected transactions unprofitable short sales and the reestablishment of successor positions using options.

An investor can avoid a wash sale simply by selling the stock and not reinvesting for thirty-one days, but she would sacrifice any appreciation on the security during that time, and conversely would be protected from any further slide in its price.

Some investors, therefore, when selling the loss position also purchase another security that they believe will "act like" the original holding. Here the investor must weigh the viability of the possible substitutes. High-grade bonds seem the most homogeneous as an asset class and the easiest to swap between, while small-cap equities seem the least interchangeable. In the real world, even blue-chip stocks in the same industry are not necessarily surrogates for each other.

Fortunately, there are ways to operate within the wash-sale rules and keep the same economic exposure, notably through certain options or a doubling-up forward conversion. These are not simple techniques; for more detail, please see Chapter 2.

Day Traders, Take a Holiday

Day traders in particular are likely to be tripped up by the rules on wash sales. That is because day traders tend to trade in and out of a few favorite holdings, only to be shocked by the whipsaw effect of the wash-sale rules at income tax time. For 2000 one investor had $1 million in profits but owed taxes on short-term gains of $3 million. He had traded two favorite stocks heavily, so that all his purchases in those stocks took place within thirty-one days of the last sale. At year-end, he had $3 million in gains on one stock and $2 million in losses on the other for a net gain of $1 million. But because of the wash-sale rules he was unable to allocate any losses against gains. Because short-term gains are taxable as ordinary income, his taxes of $1,188,000 on $3 million exceeded his actual profit of $1 million.

After year-end, there is no way to undo the whipsaw effect. However, day traders who have focused on a few stocks can avoid getting whipsawed if for the last thirty-two days of the year they close their positions and stop trading the stocks with net losses. Some traders may choose to trade securities similar to those "on hold." Others may simply take a vacation from November 30 until year-end—they are in a dream situation where they can make more money by being idle than by working.

Sell Premium Bonds to Offset Losses

Because interest rates have fallen in recent years, and bond prices rise as interest rates fall, many bond investors are sitting on portfolio gains. Therefore, in matching up gains and losses for fourth-quarter trades, consider your bond holdings as well as your equity positions.

Because the wash-sale rules apply only to losses, not to gains, you can sell a bond holding that has risen to a premium to recognize the gain and immediately buy back the same premium-priced bonds. In this case you are taking gains this year that will be offset by already realized losses. The second tax-saving opportunity this move allows is that over the coming years you can take an interest expense deduction by electing to amortize the premium on the bond (see Chapter 10).

Use a Short against the Box to Defer Taxable Gains

In doing your fourth-quarter review, suppose you discover you have a winner—a stock that has met or exceeded your objectives—that you would like to sell, but you don't want to be liable for the capital gains tax. The time-honored way to handle such a situation was to sell short against the box before the end of the year—in other words, do a short sale and cover the sale with identical securities from your portfolio next year. But the Taxpayer Relief Act of 1997 severely limited the use of this technique. Even so, you can still use it (in a limited way) to defer taxes for one year, and it works best near year-end.

As an example, assume an investor holds 800 shares of IBM that have appreciated substantially since he bought them, and he has decided to sell 200 of the shares. If he sells the shares "long," he will owe a capital gains tax. Instead, he could execute a short against the box—that is, sell 200 shares short and expressly designate the long shares that are part of the "box."

After December 31 but no later than January 30, the investor would close out the short position using long shares other than those that he designated as part of the "box." The designated shares must be held unhedged for more than sixty days after the short sale is closed. The result should be no taxable event in the current year and a sale for tax purposes in the following year. Remember that long positions are realized on their trade date, while shorts are covered on their settlement date, normally the trade date plus three. Thus for the technique to work investors can trade anytime between December 29 and January 27.

This transaction must be limited to a maximum of one-half of your position so that the proper identifications can be done. (See Chapter 5 for more details on using this technique.)

Convert Realized Capital Losses from Long Term to Short Term

In certain cases it is possible to recharacterize a realized long-term capital loss into a short-term capital loss, while potentially earning a pretax profit. You can do this by deliberately running afoul of the wash-sale rule.

Assume an investor sells at a loss a stock that he has held for more than twelve months. Within thirty days of the sale, he acquires a call option on the stock, so that he is not allowed to take the loss on that year's tax return. The amount of the loss is added to the basis of the call option, as is the holding period of the stock that was sold. If he subsequently sells the call, then he must recognize the resultant loss, though it would still be long-term.

If he exercises the call, however, and then sells the underlying stock, the tax results would be quite different. Upon the exercise of a call option, the basis of the acquired stock is equal to the strike price of the call option plus the basis in the option. The holding period of the stock begins on the date of exercise, and the holding period of the call is not added to the holding period of the stock. Therefore, if the stock is sold within twelve months of exercise, any gain or loss will be short-term. Because the loss realized on the first sale is not part of the basis in the stock of the subsequent sale, that loss takes on the character of

209

the subsequent sale. As long as the subsequent sale gives rise to a short-term capital loss, then the investor has effectively converted the long-term loss into a short-term loss. If an investor has both short-term and long-term capital gains, the loss will now offset the higher-taxed short-term gains instead of the lower-taxed long-term gains.

Designate Shares to Sell

Remember when selling part of an appreciated holding—whether a stock or a mutual fund—to designate in writing which shares you wish to sell. By selling the highest-cost shares, you can minimize any resultant capital gains tax. If you have followed our advice in Chapter 10, you have instructed your broker always to deliver the highest cost basis shares (unless notified to the contrary for a particular sale).

On the other hand, if you have taken a large loss in another issue, you may want to designate lower-cost shares because it is an opportunity to recognize a large capital gain without being taxed on it, thanks to the offsetting loss. Of course, if you are selling only part of the holding that is under water, you also need to specify which of those shares to sell. You might also want to take short-term gains if you are about to offset long-term gains with short-term losses.

Defer Income by Creating a Current Deduction

If you have net short-term gains (or other investment income) it might be possible to defer income into the next year. By making a leveraged purchase late in the year of Treasury securities with a January coupon and maturity, you should generate a deduction in the current year. In some cases the leverage can be as high as 100 to 1, making a substantial deduction for margin interest possible. As a cash-basis taxpayer you will be required to pay the interest expense to deduct it, but by the same token no income will be realized until receipt of the coupon the next year.

Review Your Mutual Funds

BECAUSE THE NATION'S SECURITIES LAWS require mutual funds to make annual distributions to shareholders of any dividends received and capital gains recognized, investors who hold funds in regular, taxable accounts must be particularly alert to what distributions may be coming. Typically, the funds make their distributions in December—and if the market has had a down year, as it did in 2000, some fund shareholders may have cashed in their holdings, forcing the fund managers to sell some securities to pay off those shareholders. If they realized gains in doing so, remaining shareholders will get a capital gains distribution, even if the overall value of their fund shares fell during the year. For more detail, please review Chapter 6.

This means that if you are a long-term investor who is considering selling fund shares, you should do so before the annual distribution. That way, your entire gain, including the amount attributable to the forthcoming distribution, will be taxed as a long-term capital gain. If you wait to sell until after the distribution has been made, it is likely that part of the distribution will be from short-term gains and dividends that are taxable as ordinary income.

If you want to buy fund shares before year-end, wait until the distribution has been made, because once it has been made, the shares' net asset value immediately falls by the amount of the distribution. If you buy before the ex-dividend date, the distribution you receive will amount to "a return of capital," but you will, nevertheless, be taxed as if you had held the shares all year. If you eventually sell the fund shares, things will more or less even out because the distribution will be added into your cost basis. A long-term investor, however, might not receive that offsetting break for many years—and if he is in a lower tax bracket then, he still will not be quite even. So it is best to avoid this trap by waiting until after the distribution to purchase shares.

Decide Whether to Exercise Your Options

IF YOU OWN OPTIONS ON YOUR employer's stock, an important year-end decision is whether to exercise them. In making that decision you want to consider both the outlook for the stock and the tax consequences of exercising the options. Generally, it is best to get professional advice on whether to exercise your options.

Remember, there are two kinds of employee options: qualified, or incentive, stock options and nonqualified stock options. When nonqualified options are exercised, the resulting income is treated as compensation income, or ordinary income, taxable at rates as high as 38.6 percent. In contrast, when qualified options are exercised, there is no current income. If the stock is held more than a year after exercise, the gain when it is sold or otherwise disposed of is treated as a long-term capital gain, taxable at a maximum rate of 20 percent. For more details, please see Chapter 11.

Therefore, if you hold nonqualified options you will usually want to exercise them as soon as you can for tax purposes, because the more the stock appreciates, the more income tax you will owe. If, after acquiring the shares, you own them at least a year, any rise in the share price from the day you bought the shares will qualify for long-term capital gains treatment.

But before acting, run the numbers on the tax consequences. If you would have to sell some of the newly acquired shares to pay your tax bill, you would have a short-term gain taxable at ordinary income rates. That would be especially galling if the transaction had pushed you into a higher tax bracket.

If you have incentive options, which are popular with technology companies, among others, you will not be liable for an immediate regular income tax on the difference between the option price and your purchase price for the stock. But these options too could set up a tax trap: the bargain element (the difference between the exercise price and the market price) is one of the so-called "preference" items that can make you liable for the AMT, so again, run the numbers before acting.

Employees who exercise options before year-end only to see the stock price then drop precipitously could wind up paying an AMT this year and have an unrealized capital loss. To avoid this situation, those employees could sell their stock in the same year of exercise.

Fund Your Retirement Plans Fully

PEOPLE WHO TAKE ADVANTAGE of tax-deferred pension plans not only build a nest egg for retirement but also hold down current adjusted gross income (AGI) and tax liabilities. A person in the top 38.6 percent tax bracket will save $4,246 on current income taxes simply by contributing the maximum allowed—$11,000 for 2002 (or $12,000 for people age fifty and over, resulting in a saving of $4,246 or $4,632, respectively, for a top-bracket taxpayer)—into an employer-sponsored 401(k) plan. In the 2001 tax law, Congress raised the limit annually to $15,000 in 2006

($20,000 for those fifty and older), allowing additional tax savings and retirement savings. Because the plans are employer-sponsored, employed persons should visit their corporate benefit offices before year-end to be sure all their paperwork is in order for the next year's deferrals. These accounts must be fully funded by year-end; contributions are not allowed to "spill over" into the next year.

The rules for other tax-deferred plans vary, as follows:

- ❏ **IRAs.** Taxpayers have until the original due date of their tax return, normally April 15, to establish and contribute to an IRA for that tax year. Contribution limits are to rise from $2,000 in 2001 to $5,000 in 2008 and from $2,000 to $6,000 for those fifty and older. Even if they file for an automatic four-month extension, they cannot extend establishing and contributing to the IRA.
- ❏ **Keogh Plans.** Self-employed persons may sock away the lesser of $30,000 or 25 percent of net self-employment income up to $170,000 in 2001 for a money-purchase plan and have until the due date of their returns, including extensions, to do so. But the plan must be set up by December 31 of the prior year. Generally, that means opening the plan and putting in some money to begin, then putting in the balance once the return has been completed and the full annual income amount is known.
- ❏ **Simplified Employee Pension Plans (SEPs).** Small businesses and sole proprietors may set up these plans through banks or brokers and contribute the lesser of 15 percent of compensation up to $170,000 or $30,000. The plans may be established and funded up to the due date of your tax return, including extensions.

Possible Drawbacks

As discussed in Chapter 7, there may also be drawbacks to any tax-deferred retirement plan: If you withdraw money before age 59½, it will be subject to ordinary income tax and will generally be subject to a 10 percent penalty as well, unless it qualifies for certain legal exceptions. When retirement distributions are made, they are taxable at ordinary income-tax rates, even if much of the account's growth came from capital gains, and you do not know now what your future income tax rate will be. These factors should be weighed along with the need to build a nest egg and to realize current tax savings by contributing to a plan.

Make Charitable Donations

SOME TAX-SAVING MOVES that are applicable year-round are, nevertheless, worth a special review at year-end, because to save taxes in the current year, you must act before December 31. One such move involves using appreciated securities for any sizable gifts to charity.

Many substantial donors wait until year-end to decide what charitable gifts to make for the year, not only to assess how well they have done during the year and thus how much they can afford to give but also to be sure they are not liable for the AMT. People who are liable for the AMT may prefer to postpone making donations until a year when they are not, when the value of a charitable deduction would be greater.

If you are among the charitably inclined and are not liable for the AMT, consider giving appreciated securities instead of cash. You get a deduction for the market value of the securities, and the charity, being tax-exempt, can sell them without being liable for capital gains tax.

Suppose, for example, you have pledged $10,000 to your alma mater. In your portfolio are 300 shares of stock now worth $50 apiece. Your cost basis is $20 a share. If you donate 200 of the shares, you get a $10,000 deduction and pay no capital gains tax. Had you sold shares to raise the $10,000 you pledged, you would have had to sell $11,364 worth to have $10,000 after paying a long-term gains tax of $1,364. Thus, by giving shares instead of writing a check to the college, you save $1,364 in taxes. But suppose you want to hold onto the shares? Donate them anyway and buy an identical holding. You will then have a higher cost basis, and that will be beneficial when you do want to sell. (Remember, the wash-sale rules apply only to losses, not to gains.)

Using appreciated securities for any charitable donations you wish to make can also be useful when you want to diversify your portfolio. Give the charity the lowest cost basis shares in a highly concentrated position and purchase a different security. This, of course, is a useful technique only for the charitably inclined. You are not going to make money by giving stock away.

TAX PLANNING NEEDS TO OCCUR both during the year and at year-end, and you should do it with an eye on the year beyond as well, lest you make a trade this year that will come back to haunt you in the following year. The one important tax-reduction move that is still available after year-end is setting up and contributing to an IRA or a SEP, if you are eligible. Otherwise, once the ball falls in Times Square, taxpayers who have failed to review their portfolios and take appropriate action will have little recourse but to pay taxes that they might have escaped by harvesting losses or using the other strategies discussed here.

Historical Tax Rates

Top Federal Individual Income-Tax Rates for Earned Income and Capital Gains

Taxable income excludes zero bracket amount from 1977 through 1986. Beginning in 1948 the rates shown apply to married persons filing joint returns. Rates are for regular income taxes and do not include either the add-on minimum tax on preference items (1970–1982) or the alternative minimum tax (1979–present). Also, they do not include the effects of the various tax benefit phaseouts (e.g. the personal exemption phaseout).

Year	TOP BRACKET Rate (percent)	Taxable Income Over (dollars)	LONG-TERM CAPITAL GAINS Top Rate (percent)	Notes on Gains Rules
1913–15	7%	$500,000	7%	Same as other income
1916	15	2,000,000	15	
1917	67	2,000,000	67	
1918	77	1,000,000	77	
1919–20	73	1,000,000	73	
1921	73	1,000,000	73	
1922	56	200,000	12.5	Top rate set at 12.5%

(continued on the following page)

	TOP BRACKET		LONG-TERM CAPITAL GAINS	
Year	Rate (percent)	Taxable Income Over (dollars)	Top Rate (percent)	Notes on Gains Rules
1923	56%	$200,000	12.5%	
1924	46	500,000	12.5	
1925–28	25	100,000	12.5	
1929	24	100,000	12.5	
1930–31	25	100,000	12.5	
1932–33	63	1,000,000	12.5	
1934–35	63	1,000,000	32	Sliding exclusion from 1 to 10 years
1936–39	79	5,000,000	39	Sliding exclusion from 18 months to 2 years
1940	81.1	5,000,000	30	
1941	81	5,000,000	30	
1942–43	88	200,000	25	
1944–45	94*	200,000	25	
1946–47	86.45*	200,000	25	
1948–49	82.13*	400,000	25	
1950	91*	400,000	25	
1951	91*	400,000	25	
1952–53	92*	400,000	25	
1954–63	91*	400,000	25	
1964	77	400,000	25	
1965–67	70	200,000	25	

Year	TOP BRACKET		LONG-TERM CAPITAL GAINS	
	Rate (percent)	Taxable Income Over (dollars)	Top Rate (percent)	Notes on Gains Rules
1968	75.25%†	$200,000	26.9%	Transition rules
1969	77†	200,000	27.5	
1970	71.75†	200,000	32.2	
1971	70‡	200,000	34.3	
1972–78	70‡	200,000	36.5–39.9	50% exclusion (surcharge in effect)
1979–80	70‡	212,000	28	60% exclusion
1981	69.125‡§	212,000	24	Transition year
1982	50	106,000	20	60% exclusion
1983	50	106,000	20	
1984	50	159,000	20	
1985	50	165,480	20	
1986	50	171,580	20	
1987	38.5	90,000	28	28% maximum set
1988	28# –33	29,750	28–33	Same as earned income
1989	28# –33	30,950	28–33	
1990	28# –33	32,450	28–33	
1991	31	82,150	28	
1992	31	86,500	28	
1993	39.6	250,000	28	
1994	39.6	250,000	28	

(continued on the following page)

Year	TOP BRACKET		LONG-TERM CAPITAL GAINS	
	Rate (percent)	Taxable Income Over (dollars)	Top Rate (percent)	Notes on Gains Rules
1995	39.6%	$256,500	28%	
1996	39.6	263,750	28	
1997	39.6	271,050	20	1997 tax law cut rate
1998	39.6	278,450	20	
1999	39.6	283,150	20	
2000	39.6	288,350	20	
2001	39.1	297,350	20	
2002–03	38.6	N.A.	20	
2004–05	37.6	N.A.	20	
2006 & later	35	N.A.	18–20	18% for property acquired in 2001 or later and held 5 years or more

* Subject to the following maximum effective rate limitations [year and maximum rate (in percent)] 1994–45 - 90; 1946–47 - 85.5; 1948–49 - 77.0; 1950 - 87.0; 1951 - 87.2; 1952–53 - 88.0; 1954–63 - 87.0.

† Includes surcharge of 7.5 percent in 1968, 10 percent in 1969, and 2.6 percent in 1970.

‡ Earned income was subject to maximum marginal rates of 60 percent in 1971 and 50 percent from 1972 through 1981.

§ After-tax credit is 1.25 percent against regular tax.

The benefit of the 28 percent bracket is eliminated by an increased rate above certain thresholds. The phaseout range of the benefit of the first rate bracket was as follows: Taxable income between $71,900 and $149,250 in 1988; taxable income between $74,850 and $155,320 in 1989; and taxable income between $78,400 and $162,770 in 1990. This added 5 percentage points to the marginal rate for those affected by the phaseout, producing a 33 percent effective rate. The phaseout of the benefit of the 28 percent bracket was repealed for taxable years beginning after December 31, 1990.

Source: Joint Committee on Taxation

APPENDIX 2

Key Points for Investors from the 2001 Tax Act

The Economic Growth and Tax Relief Reconciliation Act of 2001 is the largest tax-cut package in nearly twenty years. Some of its provisions have a direct impact on investors; others have a more indirect effect. The provisions are to be phased in gradually—in some cases the phase-in period is as long as ten years—and the law has a sunset provision for years after December 31, 2010. Because of the phase-ins and sunset provision, taxpayers will need to review and update their investments and financial plans frequently. Here are key points of the act, as it affects investors.

Income Tax Planning

FOR TAXPAYERS IN THE BRACKETS above 15 percent, the act put lower rates into effect on July 1, 2001, and the rates are to be reduced further over the following few years. Taxpayers in the highest bracket (39.6 percent in 2000) are subject to a blended rate of 39.1 percent for 2001, with their rate gradually falling to 35 percent by 2006. For the lowest-income taxpayers, the act created a new 10 percent bracket for a portion of the income that was previously taxed at 15 percent. For single people the first $6,000 of taxable income is taxed at 10 percent, effective January 1, 2001, and for married couples filing jointly, the first $12,000 is taxed at 10 percent. The following table shows how the rates are being cut:

Regular Income-Tax Rate Reductions

Calendar Year	28% Rate Cut to	31% Rate Cut to	36% Rate Cut to	39.60% Rate Cut to
2001*–2003	27%	30%	35%	38.60%
2004–2005	26	29	34	37.60
2006 and later	25	28	33	35

*Effective July 1, 2001

The act also
- ❑ Contains "marriage penalty relief provisions," which phase in gradually until 2009
- ❑ Increases the child credit to $1,000 by 2010
- ❑ Eliminates the phaseouts of itemized deductions and personal exemptions gradually until 2010. Thus in 2010, top-bracket taxpayers will not lose these breaks.

Caveat: The act does not provide relief from the Alternative Minimum Tax (AMT). In fact, by lowering regular rates and thus narrowing the spread with the AMT, it is likely to make far more taxpayers subject to the AMT. Thus, people contemplating any action that could result in an AMT liability, such as exercising stock options, should examine their situation carefully before acting.

Estate Planning

THE ACT WILL REPEAL THE ESTATE and generation-skipping transfer taxes in 2010 and in the interim gradually increases the amounts that will not be subject to those taxes and lowers rates. The unlimited deduction for bequests to a spouse remains in effect. Gifts made during a person's lifetime are to be treated differently from bequests; for 2002 onward there is a maximum applicable exclusion for lifetime gifts of $1 million.

Because substantial investors often make gifts of securities to children or grandchildren and bequeath them to heirs in their will, these provisions are important. They are also very complex, so a lawyer who specializes in trusts and estates should be consulted when planning gifts and estates. The following table shows how these provisions are to be phased in:

Estate, Generation-Skipping, and Gift Taxes

Calendar Year	ESTATE AND GST TAXES		LIFETIME GIFTS	
	Applicable Exclusion Amount	Estate and GST Tax Rate	Applicable Exclusion Amount	Highest Gift-tax Rate
2002	$1 million	50%	$1 million	50%
2003	1 million	49	1 million	49
2004	1.5 million	48	1 million	48
2005	1.5 million	47	1 million	47
2006	2 million	46	1 million	46
2007	2 million	45	1 million	45
2008	2 million	45	1 million	45
2009	3.5 million	45	1 million	45
2010	N.A. (taxes repealed)	N.A. (taxes repealed)	1 million	Top individual income tax rate

Under current law when an heir receives assets such as securities from an estate, the heir's basis is the fair market value on the decedent's date of death, not the decedent's purchase price. For an asset that the decedent had held many years, this could result in a substantial step-up in basis and, consequently, a considerable lowering of the capital gains tax that would be due when the heir sold the asset.

The 2001 Act modifies this break, effective in 2010, when estate taxes are repealed. Then, up to a total of $1.3 million in basis step-up may be allocated among transfers to any beneficiaries, and an additional $3 million of basis step-up may apply to transfers to a surviving spouse. The value of all other assets transferred at death will be based on the lesser of the decedent's adjusted basis or the fair market value on the decedent's date of death.

Retirement Planning

TAX INCENTIVES TO SAVE FOR retirement, both through IRAs and employer-sponsored plans, are significantly expanded through the act. Contribution limits are set to rise, and people aged fifty and over are allowed to contribute even more.

What is more, "portability" is being expanded—people who retire or change jobs are to have greater flexibility in transferring assets or taking them with them. Specifically:

❑   After-tax contributions to qualified retirement plans can be rolled over into IRAs.

❑   Holdings can be rolled over from an IRA into an employer-sponsored plan, such as a 401(k), 403(b), a 457 plan, or another IRA.

❑   Participants in 457, 403(b), or other qualified pension plans will be able to roll over plan assets into an IRA of another qualified retirement plan.

Annual contribution limits to both traditional and Roth IRAs are being raised gradually from $2,000 in 2001 to $5,000 in 2008 ($6,000 for people fifty and over), and limits will be subject to indexing after that. Limits for employer-sponsored plans will rise as shown in the following table:

Retirement Plans' Contribution Limits

Calendar Year	EMPLOYER-SPONSORED		SEC. 457
	Individuals Under Age 50	Individuals Age 50 and Above	Government Employees
2001	$10,500	$10,500	$8,500
2002	11,000	12,000	11,000
2003	12,000	14,000	12,000
2004	13,000	16,000	13,000
2005	14,000	18,000	14,000
2006*	15,000	20,000	15,000

*Subject to indexing in future years

The following provisions also take effect in 2002:

❑ The annual addition limit for defined-contribution plans rises to $40,000 from $35,000. There are to be subsequent increases in $1,000 increments based on the cost-of-living index.

❑ The maximum annual benefit from defined-benefit plans rises to $160,000 from $135,000.

❑ Qualified compensation limits rise to $200,000 from $170,000 with future indexing in $5,000 increments.

Education Savings

TAX BREAKS TO ENCOURAGE people to save for their children's educations are considerably enhanced. Earnings from after-tax funds deposited in both state-sponsored Section 529 Qualified State Tuition programs and Education IRAs are to be tax-free when used for qualified educational expenses. Previously, the earnings were tax-deferred. Furthermore, the annual contribution limit for Education IRAs rises to $2,000 in 2002 from the previous $500, and for consistency with other IRAs, the contribution deadline will be April 15, not December 31.

In other provisions:

❑ Contributions to both an Education IRA and a Section 529 program can now be made in the same year for the same beneficiary. That is important if, for example, parents and grandparents each want to save for the same child.

❑ The definition of qualified education expenses that may be paid tax-free from an Education IRA is being expanded to include elementary and secondary school expenses.

❑ The income phaseout range for contributions to Education IRAs is being expanded for married taxpayers filing jointly from $190,000 to $220,000, which is twice that of single taxpayers.

❑ For 2002 and 2003 single taxpayers whose adjusted gross income does not exceed $65,000 and married taxpayers filing jointly whose AGI does not exceed $130,000 may deduct up to $3,000 of qualified education expenses. For 2004 and 2005 they may deduct up to $4,000, and singles with income of $65,000 to $80,000 and couples with $130,000 to $160,000 may deduct $2,000.

Notes

Overview

1. Steven E. Landsburg, "You Too Could Face 95% Taxation," *The Wall Street Journal,* March 5, 2001, sec. A, p. 22.

Chapter 2

1. Robert E. Arnott, Andrew L. Berkin, and Jia Ye, "Loss Harvesting: What's It Worth to the Taxable Investor?" *The Journal of Wealth Management,* Spring 2001.

Chapter 3

1. There is one exception to the $3,000 annual limit for individuals. Under Section 1244 of the Internal Revenue Code, owners of small business corporations may take an annual loss of up to $50,000 a year against ordinary income—$100,000 on a joint return—for certain small-business stock. Few people can take advantage of this exception, however, because there are a number of restrictions. For example, the stock must have been issued originally to an individual or partnership for money or other property, not for stock, securities, or services, and the company that issued the stock must have issued no more than $1 million's worth.

Chapter 6

1. "Does a 'Folio' Belong in Your Portfolio?" *Business Week* online (September 12, 2000).

2. Danny Hakim, "In Gloom, a Beacon: Tax-Saving Funds," *The*

New York Times, Sunday, February 25, 2001, sec. 3, p. 8.

3. Aaron Lucchetti, "Standish Fund Payout to Carry Tax Bite," *The Wall Street Journal,* August 22, 2000, sec. C, p. 25.

4. Mark P. Hurley, president and chief executive of Undiscovered Managers, LLC; Yvonne N. Kanner, vice-president and principal of the firm; Richard H. Bregman, CFA, president of MJB Asset Management, New York; Tricia L. Duncan and Sophia R. Dowl, marketing associates and principals of Undiscovered Managers.

5. Anita Slomski, "It's Not What You Earn," *Investment Advisor,* April 2000.

Chapter 8

1. Sidney Kess and Lee Slavutin, "Planning Techniques and Tips, Qualified State Tuition Programs," CCH Inc. (January 19, 2001).

2. Carol Marie Cropper and Anne Tergesen, "College Savings Plans Come of Age," *Business Week,* March 12, 2001, 102.

Chapter 9

1. The Vanguard Group of Investment Companies, *The Vanguard Retirement Investing Guide* (New York: McGraw-Hill Companies, 1996), 153.

2. Price Waterhouse LLP, *Secure Your Future* (New York: McGraw-Hill Companies, 1996), 124.

3. Jan M. Rosen, "Building a Nest Egg," *The New York Times,* March 21, 1999, sec. 15, p. 10.

Chapter 13

1. Thomas D. Saler, "Live Free or Move," *Bloomberg Personal Finance,* May 2001, 66–77.

2. Jan M. Rosen, "Your Money: Locating Business for Tax Benefits," *The New York Times,* September 15, 1990, sec. 1, p. 32.

Glossary

Accrued interest. The interest that is due on a bond since the last interest payment was made. When the bond is sold, the buyer must pay the market price plus accrued interest.

Affiliate. Sometimes called a "control person"—an individual or entity in a position to exert direct influence on the actions of a corporation. Executive officers, directors, and owners of more than 10 percent of the voting shares are affiliates.

American Depositary Receipt (ADR). A security issued by an American bank representing foreign shares held in trust by that bank. The receipts are traded on domestic exchanges, so that American investors can buy or sell them more readily than through trades on exchanges abroad.

American Stock Exchange. The second-largest stock exchange in New York. It is where a wide variety of tax-efficient investments known as exchange-traded funds (ETFs) or "HOLDRS receipts" for specific baskets of securities, such as those in the S&P 500 stock index, are traded.

American-style option. An option that the buyer can exercise at any time between the date of purchase and the expiration date.

Arbitrage. Trading to take advantage of price differences. If, for example, ABC stock can be bought in New York for $10 a share and sold in London at $10.50, an arbitrageur may simultaneously purchase ABC shares in New York and sell the same amount in London. Arbitrage may also involve the purchase of rights or of convertible securities.

Asset. Any money, investment, or property that is owned.

Assignment. Notice to an option writer that an option holder has exercised the option. Consequently, the writer will have to deliver the security specified in the option contract.

At-risk rules. Rules that limit the amount of loss a taxpayer may deduct to the amount he or she risks losing in the activity.

At the money. Refers to an option with an exercise price equal to or very near the current price of the stock.

Auction market. The system of trading securities through brokers or agents on an exchange such as the New York Stock Exchange. Buyers compete with other buyers and sellers with other sellers.

Basis. The amount of your investment in property for tax purposes. The basis of property you buy is usually the cost. Basis is used to figure gain or loss on the sale or disposition of investment property.

Basis point. One-hundredth of a percentage point. Movements in bond yields are generally expressed in basis points. For example, if a yield falls to 5.32 percent from 5.37 percent, it has dropped 5 basis points.

Bearer bond. A bond whose issuer does not have the owner's name registered on its books.

Bid and asked. The bid is the highest price a potential buyer is willing to pay for a particular security at a given time; the asked is the lowest a seller will accept at the same time.

Block. A large stock holding or trade, generally 10,000 shares or more.

Blue-chip stock. Stock in a well-established national company that is expected to represent quality and reliability.

Bond. A debt security issued by a government, corporation, or municipality. The issuer promises to pay the bondholder a specified amount of interest for a specified length of time and to repay the principal upon maturity, or earlier if the bond is called.

Book value. The value of a stock as determined by adding all assets then deducting all debts and other liabilities and the liquidation price of any preferred issues, and then dividing the result by the number of common shares outstanding. Book value may differ widely from market value.

Broker. An agent who for a commission handles investors' orders to buy and sell securities, commodities, or other property.

Call. An option in which the holder has the right to buy a fixed amount of the underlying security at a stated price (the strike price) within a specified period of time.

Callable. A security (generally a bond or preferred shares) that may be redeemed before maturity.

Capital gain. Profits made on the sale of an asset.

Capital stock. All shares, both common and preferred, that represent ownership of a business.

Capitalization. (1) When referring to interest expense, the requirement that the expense be taken against your cost basis, rather than being taken as a current deduction for interest expense. (2) The total value of the securities issued by a corporation, including bonds, debentures, preferred and common stock, and surplus.

Cash flow. (1) The amount of money moving in and out of a transaction, thereby creating a rate of return. (2) Reported net income of a corporation plus amounts charged for depreciation, depletion, amortization, and extraordinary charges to reserves.

Cash method. An accounting method under which you report your income in the year in which you actually or constructively receive it. You generally deduct your expenses in the year you pay them.

Cashless collar. Also known as a zero-cost collar. The collar is created by buying a put and simultaneously selling an out-of-the-money call, with the strike price of the call set so that the call premium is exactly enough to pay for the cost of the put. *See* **Income-producing collar.**

Certificate of Deposit (CD). A certificate issued, generally by a bank, to a depositor who agrees to leave money on deposit for a specified period of time to earn a specific rate of interest.

Collateral. Securities or other property pledged by a borrower to secure repayment of a loan.

Commercial paper. An unsecured, short-term corporate debt instrument.

Commodities trader. A person who is actively engaged in trading contracts covered by Section 1256 of the Internal Revenue Code and is registered with a domestic board of trade that is designated as a contract market by the Commodity Futures Trading Commission.

Commodity future. A contract made on a commodity exchange, calling for the sale of a commodity at a future date for a fixed price.

Commodity Futures Trading Commission (CFTC). An agency created by Congress in 1974 to regulate exchange trading in futures.

Common stock. The shares of a company representing ownership in it. Companies also issue preferred shares, but most stock is common stock. Common stockholders are entitled to vote at a company's annual meeting.

Constructive ownership. Under the constructive ownership rules, if you own a derivative and it is referenced to a collective vehicle such as a hedge fund, the Internal Revenue Service looks through that vehicle and taxes you as though you owned the underlying asset.

Constructive sale. Section 1259 of the Internal Revenue Code sets forth conditions in which investors will be treated as having constructively sold an "appreciated financial position" by virtue of having hedged away all of the possible risk and reward. In the wake of the constructive-sale rules, collars have emerged as the most efficient way to protect stock gains without recognizing those gains. However, certain tax traps are associated with this technique. The Taxpayer Relief Act of 1997 allows collars, but it reserves the right to object to "abusive" transactions.

Conversion transaction. Any transaction entered into after April 30, 1993, that meets both of the following tests:

1. Substantially all of the expected return from the transaction is due to the time value of the net investment.
2. The transaction is one of the following:
   a. a straddle, including any set of offsetting positions on stock
   b. any transaction in which the investor acquires property (whether or not actively traded) at substantially the same time that he or she contracts to sell the same property or substantially identical property at a price set in the contract
   c. any other transaction that is marketed or sold as producing capital gains from a transaction described in (1)

Convertible. An issue that may be exchanged for another security. Generally the convertible is a bond, debenture, or preferred share that may be exchanged for common stock, usually of the same company.

Coupon bond. Bond with interest coupons attached. As the coupons become due, the bondholder presents them to receive interest payments.

Covered option. An option position that is offset by holding the underlying security.

Cumulative preferred. A stock that is given preference in dividend payments. If any dividends are omitted, cumulative preferred dividends must be paid before those on the issuer's common stock.

Day order. An order to buy or sell that expires at the end of the trading day on which it was entered if it is not executed.

Dealer. An individual or firm that buys and sells stocks and bonds as a principal rather than as an agent. A dealer may also function as a broker.

Debenture. A corporate promissory note. Usually it is backed by the general credit of a company rather than being secured by collateral.

Debit balance. The portion of the purchase price of holdings that is lent by a broker to a margin customer.

Discount. The amount by which a preferred stock or a debt issue sells below its par value. Treasury bills, for example, are sold at a discount, and holders redeem them at their face value rather than receiving interest payments per se.

Discretionary account. An account in which a broker or someone else has been given discretion by the account holder to make trades and all decisions related to the trades.

Diversification. Spreading investments among different types of holdings.

Dividend. A distribution of money or other property made by a corporation to its shareholders out of its earnings and profits.

Dividend Reinvestment Plan (DRIP). A program offered by some companies to allow stockholders to use their dividends to purchase additional shares directly from the company rather than going through a broker.

Dollar cost averaging. A disciplined system of buying a fixed dollar amount of a security or mutual fund at regular intervals. Under this system, payments buy more shares when the price is down and fewer when it is up. Thus, over time, the investor's average cost should be below the security's average price.

Economic Growth and Tax Relief Reconciliation Act of 2001. The Bush tax-cut package that will lower marginal rates, end estate taxes, and provide a variety of enhanced incentives for retirement and education savings. Most provisions are to be phased in over periods of up to ten years.

Equity flex options. Also known as E-Flex. Exchange-traded options that allow the investor to custom-tailor most contract terms, including strike price, expiration, and exercise style. E-Flex options enjoy certain tax and nontax advantages over OTC derivatives.

Equity option. Any option

1. to buy or sell stock, or
2. that is valued directly or indirectly by reference to any stock, group of stocks, or stock index.

European-style option. An option in which the buyer can exercise the contract only on the last business day prior to expiration. This style is widely used with collars.

Ex-Dividend. From the Latin: *Ex* means without. When a company declares a dividend, it makes it payable on a certain date to holders of record. When a stock is trading "ex-dividend," purchasers (under regular-way settlement) are not entitled to the dividend.

Exercise. An action by the holder of a call option to buy the underlying security or by the holder of a put option to sell it.

Exercise price. The same as a strike price: the price at which an option may be exercised.

Expiration date. The date that an option contract expires.

Ex-Rights. Without rights. To increase capital, corporations sometimes offer stockholders the right to subscribe to new or additional stock, usually at discounted prices. Someone who buys a stock selling ex-rights is not entitled to those rights.

Face value. Generally the par value of a bond, so called because it appears on the face of the bond. Market value could be higher or lower than face value, depending on the issuer's circumstances and conditions in the bond market.

Fair market value. The price at which property would change hands between a willing buyer and a willing seller, assuming both have a reasonable knowledge of the relevant facts.

529 Plans. Tax-advantaged college savings programs authorized by federal law but set up and administered by the states. The plans are named for the section of the Internal Revenue Code that authorizes them.

Flat bond. A bond whose trading price includes accrued but unpaid interest. In Australia bonds normally trade flat. Also, bonds that are in default of interest or principal are traded flat.

Forward contract. A contract to deliver a substantially fixed amount of property (including cash) for a substantially fixed price.

401(k) plans. Tax-advantaged, defined-contribution retirement plans set up by corporations for their employees. Companies often match employees' contributions in whole or in part. The plans are named for the section of the Internal Revenue Code that authorizes them.

403(b) plans. Tax-deferred annuities that function as defined-contribution pension plans for employees of public and nonprofit organizations like schools and hospitals. Again, there is often an employer match, and the plans are named for the section of the Internal Revenue Code that authorizes them.

Futures contract. An exchange-traded contract to buy or sell a specified commodity, such as wheat or coffee, or a financial instrument, such as a Treasury bond or holdings in stock indices, at a specified price at a specified future date.

General mortgage bond. A bond that is secured by a mortgage on the issuer's property; it may be outranked by another mortgage or mortgages.

Gilt-edged. High-grade. Applies to a bond issued by a company with a strong credit rating.

Good-'til-canceled (GTC) order. A standing order to buy or sell a security when it reaches a specified price; the order is good until the investor cancels it.

Government bond. A Treasury bond issued by the federal government or by a foreign government.

Growth stock. A stock that investors purchase in hope that the price will appreciate, as distinguished from an income stock, which is purchased because of its high dividend.

Hedging. The purchase, sale, or both of an option, futures contract, or other derivative to reduce or eliminate the risk in a position.

Hypothecation. Pledging securities as collateral for the debit balance in a margin account.

In the money. Refers to an option contract with intrinsic value—for example, a call option in which the underlying security is selling above the strike price, or a put option in which the underlying security is selling below the strike price.

Income stock. An issue that pays a large dividend.

Income-producing collar. A collar structured to generate positive cash flow. The collar is created by buying a put and simultaneously selling an out-of-the-money call to pay for the put and to generate a return that approximates what is available in the money market. *See Cashless collar.*

Individual Retirement Account (IRA). A tax-advantaged retirement savings plan. There are regular, or deductible, IRAs, in which the money grows on a tax-deferred basis and retirement distributions are taxed; nondeductible IRAs, for those who do not qualify for regular IRAs; and Roth IRAs, in which after-tax money is contributed. For Roths, both the earnings and the distributions generally will not be taxed.

Interest. Compensation for the use or forbearance of money. A corporation pays interest on its bonds to its bondholders.

Interest expense. Money that a borrower must pay the lender. When an investor borrows funds from his broker to buy securities, he must pay margin interest, and that expense is deductible to the extent he has investment income to offset it.

Interest income. The yield that bondholders receive or the money that is paid on a bank account or certificate of deposit. Normally, interest is taxed as ordinary income. However, most municipal bonds are tax-exempt, and interest on Treasury securities is not subject to state income tax.

Intrinsic value. The difference between an option's exercise price and the cash value of the underlying security.

Investment interest. The interest an investor paid or accrued on money borrowed that is allocable to property held for investment.

Investment portfolio. An investor's holdings.

Keogh plan. A retirement plan for self-employed people. Pretax money is invested, it grows on a tax-deferred basis, and normally distributions after age 59½ will be subject to taxes.

Leverage. For individuals, leverage generally means increasing return by investing on margin. For companies, leverage occurs when bonds or preferred shares are issued, because the bond interest or preferred-stock dividends must be paid before earnings can be attributed to common stock.

Limit order. An order to buy or sell a security when and if it reaches a specified price.

Limited partner. A partner whose participation in partnership activities is restricted and whose personal liability for partnership debts is limited to the amount of money or other property that he or she contributed or may have to contribute.

Liquidity. For individuals, cash or assets like listed stocks that can readily be converted back into cash. For the market, the ability to trade without extreme price fluctuations.

Listed option. Any option that is traded on or is subject to the rules of a qualified board or exchange.

Listed stock. The stock of a company that is traded on a securities exchange. The New York Stock Exchange cites the following as its criteria for an original listing: national interest in the company and a minimum of 1.1 million shares publicly held among no fewer than 2,000 round-lot stockholders. The publicly held common shares should have a minimum aggregate market value of $40 million, the exchange says, and the company should have net income in the latest year of more than $2.5 million before federal income tax and net income of $2 million in each of the preceding two years.

Load. A fee charged by some mutual funds for sales commissions and costs of distribution. Depending on the fund and share class, there may be a "front-end" load, charged when shares are sold; a "back-end" load, charged when they are redeemed; both; or neither.

Lock-up agreement. An agreement that restricts when an individual can dispose of his or her stock.

Long. Ownership. A person who is "long" shares owns them.

Low-basis stock. Stock that was purchased for a price that is low in comparison with its current price. Cost basis is the effective purchase price that an investor uses to compute tax liability.

Margin. The amount paid by a customer who trades using a broker's credit. Since 1974, pursuant to Federal Reserve regulations, a 50 percent margin rate has been in effect for individuals trading common stocks.

Margin call. A demand upon a customer whose equity in a margin account has declined below a minimum standard to put up money or securities with the broker.

Marked-to-market rule. The treatment of each Section 1256 contract held by a taxpayer at the close of the year as if it had been sold for its fair market value on the last business day of the year.

Market discount. The stated redemption price of a bond at maturity minus the holder's basis in the bond immediately after acquiring it. Market discount arises when the value of a debt obligation decreases after its issue date.

Market discount bond. Any bond having market discount except:
1. short-term obligations with fixed maturity dates of up to one year from the date of issue;
2. tax-exempt obligations that you bought before May 1, 1993;
3. U.S. savings bonds; and
4. certain installment obligations.

Market order. An order to buy or sell a security at the prevailing market price.

Maturity date. The date that a bond will come due.

Monetize. To borrow against. Monetization allows an investor to create a cash balance without liquidating the stock.

Money market account or fund. An account or mutual fund in which the assets are invested in short-term instruments, such as Treasury bills and commercial paper. It is considered a cash equivalent.

Mortgage bond. A bond secured by a mortgage on a property.

Municipal bond. A bond, generally tax-exempt, issued by a state, county, city, district, or authority. However, certain municipal bonds are not tax-exempt for taxpayers who are subject to the alternative minimum tax.

Mutual fund. The popular name for an investment company. By investing in mutual funds individuals can achieve diversity and, except in the case of index funds, get professional management. Shares of open-end funds are sold or redeemed at net asset value (NAV). Closed-end funds generally trade like stocks and often sell at a discount to NAV.

Naked option. An option position that is not offset by owning the underlying security.

Nasdaq. An automated quotation system developed by the NASD. Nasdaq, the world's first electronic stock market, is the fastest-growing major stock market in the world and is home to more than half the companies traded on the primary markets in the United States. Because trading is executed through a computer and telecommunications network, which rapidly transmits data around the globe rather than on an exchange floor, a virtually unlimited number of market participants can trade in companies' stocks. This gives companies greater access to investors and increased visibility in the market.

National Association of Securities Dealers (NASD). The national association of securities brokers and dealers.

Net asset value (NAV). Usually used in connection with mutual funds. The net asset value is the total market value of all securities owned less all liabilities. The net asset value per share is that balance divided by the number of shares outstanding.

Net change. The change in the price of a security from one closing price to another. It may be for a day, week, year, or any holding period.

New issue. A stock or bond sold by a company for the first time.

New York Stock Exchange (NYSE). The largest organized securities market in the United States, founded in 1792. The exchange describes itself as "a not-for-profit corporation of 1,366 individual members, governed by a Board of Directors consisting of twelve public representatives, twelve member firm representatives, and a full-time chairman, executive vice chairman, and president." It adds, "The Exchange itself does not buy, sell, own, or set the price of securities traded there. The prices are determined by the public supply and demand."

Noncumulative. A type of preferred stock on which dividends that are skipped do not accrue.

Nonequity option. Any listed option that is not an equity option, such as debt options, commodity futures options, currency options, and broad-based stock index options.

Odd lots. Stock transactions of fewer than 100 shares.

Open interest. For options and futures, the number of outstanding contracts that have not been exercised and have not yet expired.

Option. The right to buy or sell a fixed amount of a security at a specified price within a specified period of time. If the right is not exercised before the option expires, the buyer forfeits the cost of the option. American-style options can be exercised any time after purchase and before their expiration date; European-style options are exercised on the last day of business before their expiration date. E-flex options are exchange-traded options that allow the investor to custom-tailor most contract terms, including strike price, expiration, and exercise style.

Options dealer. Any person registered with an appropriate national securities exchange as a market maker or specialist in listed options.

Orders. Instructions for handling transactions, such as an order to buy 100 shares at market or to sell 1,000 shares at a minimum price of $50 per share.

Original-issue discount (OID). The amount by which the stated redemption price at maturity of a debt instrument is more than its issue price.

Out of the money. Refers to an option that has no intrinsic value—for example, a put option in which the stock is selling above the exercise price or a call option in which the stock is selling below the exercise price.

Over-the-counter (OTC). A market in which securities transactions are conducted off the floor of an exchange. The terms of these transactions are privately negotiated and entered into between the investor and dealer. Dealers may or may not be members of a securities exchange as well.

Paper profit or loss. An unrealized profit or loss on a security in one's portfolio.

Par. The nominal or face value of a security.

Passive activity. The conduct of a trade or business in which you do not materially participate, including rental activity. However, the rental of real estate is not a passive activity if both of the following are true:

1. More than one-half of the personal services you perform during the year in all trades or businesses are performed in real property trades or businesses in which you materially participate.

2. You perform more than 750 hours of services during the year in real property trades or businesses in which you materially participate.

Point. The meaning varies. For stock, a point means $1. For bond prices, a point means $10, since a bond is quoted as a percentage of $1,000. A bond that rises 3 points gains 3 percent of $1,000, or $30, in value. Changes in bond yields are often expressed in basis points, which are one-hundredth of a percentage point. When a bond's price rises, its yield drops; if it falls to 5.27 percent from 5.32 percent, it has lost 5 basis points. For market indices, the word point simply refers to a numerical change in the index, not to dollars or percents. If the Dow Jones Industrial Average climbs to 11,150 from 11,100, it has gained 50 points.

Portfolio. A person's or an institution's securities holdings.

Portfolio income. Gross income from interest, dividends, annuities, or royalties that is not derived in the ordinary course of a trade or business. It includes gains from the sale or trade of property (other than an interest in a passive activity) producing portfolio income or held for investment.

Preferred stock. A class of stock that is more conservative than common stock in that owners take precedence in assets and earnings in the event of liquidation or dividend payments. Preferred stock generally does not carry voting rights, however, and is more like a bond than a stock.

Premium. For bonds or preferred stock, the amount by which an issue sells above its par value. If the issue is redeemed above its face value, it is redeemed at a premium. For options, a premium is the price that the buyer pays the writer for the contract.

Prepaid variable forward. A type of forward sale contract in which the investor receives an up-front payment in exchange for a commitment to deliver securities in the future, with the number of shares to be delivered varying with the underlying share price.

Prime rate. Originally, the interest rate banks charged their largest, most creditworthy corporate customers, although such corporate clients may often be able to negotiate even lower rates. Still, banks officially maintain a prime rate, and it is often used as a benchmark for setting rates on personal, automobile, commercial, and financing loans.

Principal. (1) The person for whom a broker executes an order, or dealers buying or selling for their own accounts. (2) A person's capital. (3) The face amount of a bond.

Private activity bond. A bond that is part of a state or local government bond issue of which:

1. more than 10 percent of the proceeds are to be used for a private business use, and
2. more than 10 percent of the payment of the principal or interest is
   a. secured by an interest in property to be used for a private business use (or payments for the property), or
   b. derived from payments for property (or borrowed money) used for a private business use.

Profit-taking. Selling appreciated securities to realize a profit. Market downturns after a period of rising prices are often attributed to profit-taking when there is no ready business or economic explanation for the shift.

Put. An option in which the holder has the right to sell a fixed amount of the underlying security at a stated price (the strike price) within a stated period of time.

Rate of return. Yield, the annualized percentage return investors earn on their holdings.

Real estate investment trust (REIT). An exchange-traded issue that represents a portfolio of real estate investments. REITs are required to distribute as much as 90 percent of their income, so REIT investors are often people who are seeking current income.

Real estate mortgage investment conduit (REMIC). An entity that holds a fixed pool of mortgages secured by interests in real property, with multiple classes of interests held by investors. These interests may be either regular or residual.

Record date. The date on which a shareholder must be registered to receive any dividend declared or to vote at a company's annual meeting.

Redemption price. The price at which an issuing company may redeem a bond before maturity. Certain types of preferred stock may also be redeemed.

Refinancing or refunding. The sale of new securities by a company to retire existing securities, often to save interest costs or to extend maturities.

Registered bond. A bond that is registered in the owner's name with the issuing company. It cannot be transferred unless endorsed by the registered owner.

Registered representative. Generally an employee of a brokerage firm who serves as an account executive for customers and who has passed qualifying securities examinations and is registered with the SEC.

Registration. New securities to be offered to the public must be registered with the SEC by the issuer. A registration statement must disclose information about the company's operations, securities, and management and the purpose of the public offering. A security must also be registered before it may be traded on a national exchange.

Regulated futures contract. A Section 1256 contract that

1. provides that amounts that must be deposited to or may be withdrawn from your margin account depend on daily market conditions (a system of marking to market), and

2. is traded on or is subject to the rules of a qualified board of exchange, such as a domestic board of trade designated as a contract market by the Commodity Futures Trading Commission or any board of trade or exchange approved by the Secretary of the Treasury.

Regulation T. The Federal Reserve Board regulation that governs the extension of credit by brokerage firms to customers for the purpose of purchasing or carrying additional securities.

Regulation U. The federal regulation governing the amount of credit that banks may extend to customers to buy listed stock.

Restricted stock. Stock you receive that cannot be traded on the public markets for a specified period of time.

Round lot. A holding or block of shares in a multiple of 100 shares.

Secondary market. After an issuer sells stocks or bonds, any subsequent trading—that is, most securities transactions—takes place on the secondary market.

Section 1256 contract. Any

1. regulated futures contract,

2. foreign currency contract as defined in Chapter 4 under Section 1256 Contracts Marked to Market,

3. nonequity option, or

4. dealer equity option.

Securities and Exchange Commission (SEC). A watchdog agency established by Congress in the 1930s to help protect investors by administering federal securities laws.

Securities Investors Protection Corporation (SIPC). A nonprofit membership corporation created by an Act of Congress to insure investors' capital in case a brokerage firm fails. The SIPC, which is a counterpart to the FDIC for bank deposits, insures up to $500,000 of cash and securities per customer.

Serial bond. An issue that matures at periodic stated intervals.

Settlement. Conclusion of a securities transaction, when a customer pays for securities purchased or delivers securities sold and receives the proceeds of the sale from a broker.

Short covering. Buying stock to repay borrowed stock to make delivery on a short sale.

Short position. The total amount of stock an investor has sold short and has not covered as of a given date. Also, stock options or futures contracts sold short and not covered as of a particular date.

Short sale. The sale of a borrowed security. The seller generally expects the security's price to decline and thus that he will be able to repay the loan with lower-priced shares. Sometimes people sell short a stock they already own to protect a paper profit. This is known as selling short against the box, a practice that was limited by but not halted by the Taxpayer Relief Act of 1997.

Sole proprietorship. A business that is owned and operated by one person.

Specialist. A stock exchange member who has two primary functions: first, to maintain an orderly market in the securities assigned to him by buying or selling for his own account when necessary; and second, to act as a broker's broker for stop or limit orders.

Split. The division of a corporation's outstanding shares into either a larger or smaller number of shares. For example, if a stock trading at $50 is split 2-for-1, a shareholder with 100 shares valued at $5,000 would then have 200 shares, still valued at $5,000, or $25 each. A reverse split would reduce the number of shares outstanding and mean each share would be worth more.

Stock dividend. A dividend paid in securities rather than in cash.

Stock index futures. Futures contracts based on market indices.

Stockholder of record. A stockholder whose name is registered with the issuing corporation.

Stop order. An order to buy a stock at a price above or sell at a price below the current market, generally to limit a loss or protect unrealized profits on a short sale.

Straddle. Generally, a set of offsetting positions on personal property. A straddle may consist of a security and a written option to buy and a purchased option to sell on the same number of shares of the security, with the same exercise price and period.

Straddle rules. Internal Revenue Code Section 1092 defines and governs straddles. Under the straddle rules, when a position is deemed to be part of a straddle, any loss realized from closing one leg is deferred to the extent there is any unrealized gain on the open leg; however, any gain realized from closing a leg of a straddle must be recognized immediately. Interest expense incurred to "carry a straddle" must be capitalized, as opposed to being currently deductible. Straddle rules apply to positions in stock established after December 31, 1983.

Street name. The name on securities held in the name of a broker instead of in the name of a customer. Unlike past generations of investors, who stored stock certificates in safe-deposit boxes and delivered the certificates to brokers when they sold shares, most investors today want their brokers to hold their securities for safety and to facilitate trading.

Strike price. Also called *exercise price.* The price at which the stock or commodity underlying a call option or a put option can be purchased or sold over a specified period.

Stripped preferred stock. Stock that meets the following tests:

1. There has been a separation in ownership between the stock and any dividend on the stock that has not become payable.
2. The stock
   a. is limited and preferred as to dividends,
   b. does not participate in corporate growth to any significant extent, and
   c. has a fixed redemption price.

Swap. A contractual agreement under which the two parties exchange payments based on the price changes and distributions from a security, as well as the cost to carry the security. A swap investor can retain all the upside and downside potential of a stock but get to keep the cash that would have been tied up in the investment. The net cost of the swap is the difference between the interest earned on the dollars kept and the "interest" charged on the notional amount of the contract.

Swapping. Selling one security, generally to recognize a tax loss, and buying a similar one almost at the same time to maintain the position in a portfolio.

Taxpayer Relief Act of 1997 (TRA '97). Among other provisions, TRA '97 added Code Section 1259, titled "Constructive Sales Treatment for Appreciated Financial Positions." The constructive-sale rule significantly altered conditions for hedging and monetizing low-basis equity positions. *See Constructive sale.*

Third market. Over-the-counter trading of securities listed on a stock exchange by brokers who are not exchange members.

Time value. The part of an option premium that exceeds its intrinsic value.

Trader. (1) Individuals who buy and sell primarily for short-term profit are often considered "traders," although the IRS, with court backing, has been loath to recognize them as traders if their transactions are strictly for their own accounts. (2) An employee of a broker-dealer or financial institution who buys and sells securities for the firm and/or its clients.

Treasuries. Debt obligations—that is, bills, notes, and bonds—issued by the United States government. The interest on Treasuries is exempt from state and local taxes but is subject to federal income tax.

Treasury stock. Stock issued by a company but later reacquired and held in the company's treasury. It may be held indefinitely, reissued to the public, or retired. Treasury stock does not receive dividends, and it carries no voting rights.

Triple witching hour. The last trading hour on the third Friday of March, June, September, and December. That is when options and futures on stock indices expire.

Turnover rate. The volume of shares traded in a year as a percentage of total shares listed. It applies to shares traded and outstanding for an individual issue or held in an institutional portfolio.

Underlying. The security that an option holder has the right to buy or sell according to the contract terms.

Unlisted stock. A stock that is not listed on an exchange.

Variable annuity. A tax-advantaged supplemental retirement investment, essentially a clone of a popular mutual fund sold with a life-insurance wrapper. How much the policyholder receives during retirement will depend on the performance of the stock portfolio.

Warrant. A certificate giving the holder the right to buy securities at a stipulated price, either within a specified time or in perpetuity. A warrant may be offered with securities as an inducement to buy.

Wash sale. A sale of stock or securities at a loss within thirty days before or after the holder buys or acquires substantially identical stock or securities in a fully taxable trade or acquires a contract or option to buy such stock or securities.

When issued. A shortened form of "when, as, and if issued." The term indicates a conditional transaction in a security that has been authorized for issuance but has not yet been issued.

Writer. A person who sells an option, assuming the obligation to sell or buy the underlying security if the option is exercised.

Yield. The dividends or interest that investors receive on their stocks and bonds as a percentage of the holdings' value. Also known as *rate of return.*

Yield to maturity. Applies to bonds. The yield of a bond to maturity is greater than the current yield when the bond is selling at a discount to its face value and less than the current yield when the bond is selling at a premium to par.

Zero-coupon bond. A bond that is issued at a discount to its redemption price. Although it pays no current interest, generally interest is imputed annually, which tends to make the bonds more attractive for tax-exempt or tax-deferred accounts than for regular accounts.

Index

About Bloomberg

Bloomberg L.P., founded in 1981, is a global information services, news, and media company. Headquartered in New York, the company has 9 sales offices, 2 data centers, and 79 news bureaus worldwide.

Bloomberg, serving customers in 100 countries around the world, holds a unique position within the financial services industry by providing an unparalleled range of features in a single package known as the BLOOMBERG PROFESSIONAL™ service. By addressing the demand for investment performance and efficiency through an exceptional combination of information, analytic, electronic trading, and Straight Through Processing tools, Bloomberg has built a worldwide customer base of corporations, issuers, financial intermediaries, and institutional investors.

BLOOMBERG NEWS℠, founded in 1990, provides stories and columns on business, general news, politics, and sports to leading newspapers and magazines throughout the world. BLOOMBERG TELEVISION®, a 24-hour business and financial news network, is produced and distributed globally in seven different languages. BLOOMBERG RADIO™ is an international radio network anchored by flagship station BLOOMBERG® WBBR 1130 in New York.

In addition to the BLOOMBERG PRESS® line of books, Bloomberg publishes *BLOOMBERG® MARKETS, BLOOMBERG PERSONAL FINANCE™,* and *BLOOMBERG® WEALTH MANAGER.* To learn more about Bloomberg, call a sales representative at:

Frankfurt:	49-69-92041-200	São Paulo:	5511-3048-4530
Hong Kong:	85-2-2977-6600	Singapore:	65-212-1200
London:	44-20-7330-7500	Sydney:	61-2-9777-8601
New York:	1-212-318-2200	Tokyo:	81-3-3201-8950
San Francisco:	1-415-912-2980		

FOR IN-DEPTH MARKET INFORMATION and news, visit BLOOMBERG.COM®, which draws from the news and power of the BLOOMBERG PROFESSIONAL™ service and Bloomberg's host of media products to provide high-quality news and information in multiple languages on stocks, bonds, currencies, and commodities, at **www.bloomberg.com**.

About the Authors

Robert N. Gordon is the president of Twenty-First Securities Corporation, which provides investment advice and financial management for corporate, institutional, and individual clients. He was formerly the partner in charge of risk and tax arbitrage at Oppenheimer & Company and chairman of the Securities Industry Association's Tax Policy Committee. Mr. Gordon also is an adjunct professor at New York University's Graduate School of Business and serves on the board of the Securities Industry Foundation for Economic Education.

Jan M. Rosen, a long-time editor and former columnist (*Your Money* and *Tax Watch*) in the financial news department of *The New York Times,* has been responsible for that newspaper's annual tax section for many years. In addition, she is a contributor to *Tax Hotline* and other newsletters published by Boardroom, Inc. Ms. Rosen holds a bachelor's degree from Trinity University in San Antonio, Texas, and a master's degree from Columbia University in New York, where she attended the Graduate School of Journalism.